VICTORIAN LONDON

Priscilla Metcalf

CASSELL · LONDON

CASSELL & COMPANY LTD
35 Red Lion Square, London WC1R 4SG
Sydney, Auckland
Toronto, Johannesburg

First published 1972

I.S.B.N. 0 304 29049 1

Photoset and Printed by BAS Printers Limited, Wallop, Hampshire
F.772

*For Eleanor and Tom Greeves of Bedford Park
and the memory of R. Affleck Greeves*

Contents

Illustrations

Preface

Victorian London in this series must be more selective than, say, *Roman London*. We know so much more about it. Yet even a highly condensed account of its fabric and flavour must be more than a re-creation of time and place, because Victorian London was also a state of mind. As reinterpreted by Victorians in that self-conscious age, the London scene of innumerable historical events, the London setting for innumerable works of art and literature, the London echoing in innumerable periodicals, set up a world-idea of the place that has existed ever since; an idea now worn somewhat thin, as old fabrics and assumptions crumble. But it is important to understand the Victorian fabric in all its variousness. Churchill was to say in 1943, on the subject of restoring the bombed House of Commons chamber to its old rectangularity, 'We shape our buildings and afterwards our buildings shape us.' The cities Victorians left behind them have been shaping us.

I have tried to give some sense of total surroundings, the context of Victorian Londoners' lives, even those parts not Victorian-made but inherited, because some of these inherited arenas of city life went on being active parts of the fabric right down the century and after, and form part of our idea of the place. Arrested pieces of the old Georgian fabric, even fragments of the Caroline, Tudor, and medieval fabric, washed with six decades of Victorian life, became part of the world-idea of Victorian London.

Cold roast Victorian, with neither the slums nor the poetry, is sometimes what architectural historians serve up. Yet the human facts behind London's vast property network, both the big pieces of land ownership in the middle and the infinite mosaic of the suburbs, have a poetry too. Melbury Road without Lombard Street doesn't make sense, nor vice versa. And slums boiled in the background as the polluted River Thames did, together the worst exploitation of man's environment and of man himself that the world had then seen. And so a summary account of London's fabric and flavour from 1837 to 1901 must be an unholy mixture. While my arrangement of chapters by decades is an artificial division of the flow of time, it is no more so than the biographer's division of his subject into chapters; the device of the decade is the century-biographer's chapter device. The little coda of post-Victorian postcard messages preserves a few common themes left over from the Late Victorian chorus.

Inevitably such a summary is compiled partly secondhand. 'So many-sided is London, so numerous are the points of inquiry it presents, so enormous and weighty the interests involved, that it needs many endeavours before the whole can be grasped,—the co-operation of many minds before much can be effected' (*Builder*, 3 October 1857). Though I owe very much to many specialist writers and reference librarians, some of the material here from Victorian records and all of it from Victorian periodicals, was dredged up by me. Thumbnail sketches of ordinary Londoners here and there were worked up from ordinary public records (and corrections will be welcomed). There is a minimum of administrative history, in view of the history of London now in the course of publication under the editorship of Francis Sheppard, as well as the *Survey of London* volumes also edited by him.

I owe special gratitude to Sir Nikolaus Pevsner and to Sir John Summerson for ploughing through a long University of London thesis from which a little has rubbed off on this book, and to the University of Leicester for giving me a three-year research fellowship in Victorian Studies. Sir James Richards has helped with much-appreciated editorial advice. Peter Jackson has been tremendously helpful with illustrations. Directories in the Greater London Council's Members' Library and the Guildhall Library, and records and periodicals in the Minet Library and the Battersea (now Wandsworth) Reference Library were uniquely informative. And without the London Library and the Library of the Royal Institute of British Architects I could not have managed at all.

Victorian London books proliferate hourly, far too many to mention, but a few important ones are listed at the end. The chief museum collections are of course the Victoria and Albert Museum, the London Museum, and, wherever it may finally find itself, the Transport Museum now in Clapham. But one's primary source must be the streets of London. Everyone interested in the London environment should join, first their local amenity society, and then the Victorian Society (29 Exhibition Road, London SW7), which can be a potent force for intelligent conservation of the good that is left to us, so long as we support it.

And finally I should like to pay anxious tribute to that threatened institution the London bus, not just because it flowered in Victorian London, but because I could never have inspected the far-flung remains without it and persist in the belief that the London bus, supplemented by stout feet and fatalism about time and the weather, is better than any new-fangled aid to that Victorian pleasure, sight-seeing.

P.M.

Wandsworth Common

CHAPTER ONE

The Fabric of London in 1837

The first year of the Victorian Age opened with scenes from the Dark Ages. The springtime of a new reign, heralded by two carriages speeding across Middlesex in the dawn of June 20 from the old king's death chamber at Windsor toward the sleeping princess at Kensington came, like all springtimes, out of decay.

In January, the aftermath of heavy Christmas snowfall had been a violent epidemic of influenza: 'Death had a high day in the metropolis last Sunday' (the 15th, said the *Annual Register*), hearses and mourning coaches hurried from one funeral to another, scenes in the combined churchyards of St Pancras and St Giles were 'truly awful', the ground looked like a 'ploughed field', knots of mourners with their dead stood about waiting for the clergyman to finish the one before, navvies hired as gravediggers expressed their feelings in 'awful language' as they jumped and stamped on the coffins to force them into the earth. No wonder old Sir John Soane, who died in his museum of a house on the 20th, was not laid in his tomb in St Giles churchyard until the 30th. Future disturbance of this outlying burial ground by the Midland Railway, in the Sixties, was unimaginable; yet half a mile westward, north of Euston Square, a railway earthquake was swallowing up long pieces of the frowzy fields called Staggs's Gardens in *Dombey and Son*, while the Duke of Bedford developed the rest.

The overcrowding of London's dead, even unassisted by epidemics, became a matter of Government concern before overcrowding of the living did, and was already leading to the creation of more distant cemetery-suburbs. Kensal Green had been authorized in 1832 (year of cholera), Norwood in 1836, with Highgate, Abney Park, Brompton, Nunhead, and Tower Hamlets soon after. Yet

1

housefuls of the living still hummed within sound of Bow Bells, and were to be roused at dawn on Victoria's coronation day by a salvo of artillery from the Tower. That may not have roused the very poor in the stinking courts of Holborn and Whitechapel or the warrens near Westminster Abbey, where little sound or light or sense can have penetrated from outside, and people lived and died in a world of their own 'in the midst of . . . an opulent, spirited and flourishing community', as investigators for a parliamentary committee were about to discover.

Statistics on the number of people in London depended on how you defined its area. 'London' properly meant the ancient square mile of the City of London; 'the Metropolis' was the term used during most of Victoria's reign for the whole built-up area around it and including it, with borders variously defined for the registration of births and deaths, the postal delivery, the powers of the Metropolitan Police, or parliamentary representation, but containing in 1837 more than a million and a half people, nearer two million probably, although between one national census and the next precisely how many was impossible to assess. Mainly situated in Middlesex, London reached into Essex and Surrey and Kent. Besides the cities of London and Westminster and the borough of Southwark, there were the new parliamentary boroughs of Marylebone, Finsbury, Tower Hamlets, Lambeth, and Greenwich, and endless suburbs in ribbons and clusters. The whole formed 'the city of the greatest ascertained population, and the greatest number of houses, in the world', Londoners assured themselves.

This was the Modern Babylon—that much-used Victorian phrase adapted from Byron, as Paris to its poets was *Babylone*—Cowper's 'opulent, enlarged, and still/Increasing London! Babylon of old/ Not more the glory of the earth than she'. The warning spirit of 'one with Nineveh and Tyre. . . . Lest we forget' was implicit in the name, long before Kipling and the Diamond Jubilee:

> One cannot . . . reflect upon it as a whole, without feelings, almost, of awe. London . . . the central spot in the civilized globe. . . . Let us not, however be led away to vanity; for almost equally great were the cities of Babylon, and Nineveh, and Palmyra, and Tyre. (George Godwin, *The Churches of London*, vol. I, 1838, on St Bartholomew's by the Royal Exchange)

'Vast' was the word so often applied to London. Any city then was scaled to the pace of a horse. Even if the best horses drawing a fast mail-coach on the best open roads would travel at twelve miles per hour, cart-horses drawing a wagon of merchandise through heavy traffic in narrow city streets from, say, St Katharine's Docks to Hammersmith, over eight miles, took all day. Traffic surveys, then as now, were made in Oxford Street, to discover at the beginning of 1839 that 7,000 vehicles passed the corner of Newman Street in the eighteen hours between six a.m. and midnight (only about six per minute, but soon to double and triple); of these more than 1,000 were omnibuses, single-deck affairs with no roof-passengers. The hansom cab and the four-wheeler cab had been invented, but there were still more hackney coaches than buses on the road (although by 1845 Thackeray wrote a piece for *Punch*, 'Where have the hackney coaches gone to?'). Much of the population went about its business on foot. A mute witness to the traffic of porters carrying loads on their heads or shoulders survives in the 'porter's rest' re-erected at the west end of Piccadilly, south side, a stout plank supported at shoulder height by two iron columns. In June, girls walked in from the strawberry beds of Hammersmith and Fulham with baskets of hautbois (pronounced and sometimes spelled hoboys, a kind of strawberry) on their heads, filling the air with their street-cry: 'Hautbois! fresh-gather'd! taste and try! Hautbois! ripe hautbois! come and buy!' Gavarni, the French artist, was to draw them for the *Illustrated London News* in 1849. Many of the 'tribes of London' ordinarily moved out of their own districts very little: 'For the various portions of the earth are not more distinct, as regards their aborigines, than the many quarters of London, each to each', observed *Puck* (a rival of *Punch*) a few years later.

Part of London's vastness-effect lay in its situation in a broad river basin: the traveller approaching by road from north, south, east or south-west was presented with a view of it from the heights of Highgate or Banstead Downs or Blackheath or Wandsworth. The approach by river had its own views (*Fig. 1*). But when the trains came, their entry was to be intrusive, their view myopic, of grimy third-floor backs and chimney-pots, or of basements marooned on precipices.

All winter London lay under its usual pall of chimney-smoked river-basin mist, 'the sublime canopy that shrouds the City of the World', Haydon the painter called it. The sight of it 'hanging in gloomy grandeur over the vastness of our Babylon' always filled his mind with 'feelings of energy such as no other spectacle could inspire': standing on Primrose Hill or Greenwich Hill, one could

Fig. 1 *London on Thames, after a drawing by W. H. Bartlett*

catch a glimpse of the dome of St Paul's, 'announcing at once civilisation and power'. A fashionable shade for women's dresses, as 1837 dawned, was a squirrel-grey called London Smoke—half a generation earlier, in the classically-minded Twenties, called Dust of Ruins. The clothes and faces of the poor, too, wore this shade.

The January thaw that ushered in the germs and hopes of 1837, melting December's great drifts in a stew of mud, uncovered the London collection of building materials—soot-darkened bricks of brown and yellow clay and some ageing red; soot-streaked white and yellow and grey stone; and the latest stucco skins, coatings that later Victorians were to call 'compounds of wattle and daub and lucifer matches' (chimney-flues and bed-curtains being common sources of fires). Ranges of this or that building material, like rings in old tree trunks, recorded London's growth, its widening rings of spontaneous construction. Most of the domestic buildings in use in 1837 were, in the City, post-1666 brick and stonework with some older half-timbering beyond the skirts of the Great Fire; south of Oxford Street, early eighteenth-century brick and stonework, and north of Oxford Street late eighteenth-century brickwork and early nineteenth-century parti-stuccoed brick rows ending to northward in green fields; the Regent Street vein of pale stucco ran around Regent's Park; and the market gardens between Knightsbridge and the river were partly sown with Mr Cubitt's solid new houses. In Westminster as in Holborn and eastward were slums (a cant word then with many meanings, including ours). The first official investigation (1837–8) of this phenomenon under everyone's nose discovered with surprise the sanitary conditions that produced 'typhus, and the fevers which proceed from the malaria of filth'. Many a non-slum house sat upon its own cesspool, linked neither to drain nor sewer. 'Night men' with carts removed the residue. Other houses were connected to a patchwork of sewers of a sort, some drained to open ditches, and all drainage that drained at all ran eventually in this river valley into the Thames.

Nothing 'Victorian' of course existed (the adjective seems first to have come into use for architecture late in the Fifties); although a Victoria Square near the stables of the new Buckingham Palace was soon to be named for the young Queen. In 1837 London's full set of garden squares was far from complete. For instance, in Eaton Square, begun in 1828, building went on up to 1855, though the Belgrave Square houses were almost all occupied by 1837 (a light-hearted Late Victorian was to compare 'the old turret ships to a side of Belgrave Square going out for a sail'). St George's Square, London's only residential square open to the river at one end (perhaps a thought from Brighton), was laid out at first in 1839 as two streets, then in 1843 as a square with a steamer pier, and building there went on mainly from the Fifties until 1874. A similar pattern of development went on in Bayswater, like Belgravia garbed in stucco, 'pale and polite' districts where mansions were 'painted a faint whitey-brown' (Thackeray on Snobs)—like Belgravia's 'sallow squares', where people prepared for evenings 'six parties deep' (Henry James).

Parliament Square had been partially formed before Waterloo. Between Old and New Palace Yard and the muddy riverbank in 1837 stood the uncleared ruins of the old Palace of Westminster, spectacularly burned down in 1834 except for its ancient Hall, the ruins much sketched by artists and antiquaries while the first contracts were being drawn up to embank the river in preparation for foundations of momentous new buildings. The competition of 1835 for new Houses of Parliament could be called the first modern architectural competition in England. The winner is said to have

5

grown up beside the site as child of a stationer in Bridge Street, near the approach to Westminster Bridge, and as articled pupil to a Lambeth surveyor just over the bridge. If site-sense helps to win competitions, Charles Barry had it. His and the other competing designs were exhibited in 1836 in the unfinished National Gallery (still surrounded by hoardings and the dome not completed), in the eastern rooms reserved for the Royal Academy. Barry's first design had low roofs; the idea of romantic steep roofs occurred to him a little later. In a sense, the New Palace of Westminster was the first Victorian building (*Fig. 2*).

Trafalgar Square, already cleared and named, stood empty. The National Gallery, that much-maligned building (1834–8)—a favourite Victorian butt for having fulfilled an inadequate brief, on its inadequate mews-site, in an outmoded neo-classical style—lay across the top of the untreated slope like a noble retaining wall. Other neo-classical buildings of the Twenties and Thirties, Morley's Hotel and the Royal College of Physicians, formed the eastern and western

Fig. *2 The Houses of Parliament, as completed 1860*

sides of the new square, while the southern funnel of Charing Cross draining into Whitehall was lined partly by cramped little four-storey buildings with shops below and warehousing or living quarters above, partly by the long Jacobean brick-and-stone front of Northumberland House. Before the new square was cleared, a grubby congeries of houses and inns—including the Golden Cross Inn from which issued Mr Pickwick and party—had clustered about the church of St Martin-in-the-Fields and the old open space spread before the Royal Mews, and had inspired by their destruction in the early Thirties that modern-sounding dirge (attributed to Maginn of *Fraser's Magazine*):

> Oh, London won't be London long,
>   For 'twill be all pulled down;
> And I shall sing a funeral song
>   O'er that time-honoured town.

A new layout for the undeveloped central space was to be a Victorian affair.

At the end of April 1837 the old King, as one of the last public acts of his life, opened the Royal Academy's first Summer Exhibition held in the new rooms on Trafalgar Square (although the National Gallery itself was opened by the new Queen a year later). The keys so grandly presented to him on the front steps had only just arrived from Birmingham, but not by rail—the line from Euston as far as Boxmoor was to be opened in July. One of the exhibits, indeed, was Philip Hardwick's drawing for the principal entrance, 'now erecting', to the Euston Square terminus of the London & Birmingham Railway; the so-called Euston Arch with 'columns of gigantic girth opened a vista to the railway world beyond' (*Dombey and Son*). Seen by some people at the time as the gateway to a new age, by others as a blown-up travesty upon the Doric order, it was pulled down for no good reason in 1962. It reached a sort of apotheosis ten years after it was begun, in March 1847, when the actors, elephants, camels and horses of a Mammoth Troupe, having just arrived at the Euston Terminus for a performance at Drury Lane, put on all its costumes and music, and proceeded splendidly through the mammoth portico as a street spectacle and walking advertisement, and on via Piccadilly to its quarters in Farringdon Street. Nothing grander can have proceeded through the Euston gateway thereafter. A witness to the gateway's grand scale is one of its guttae—the smallest, peglike elements in the Doric order—almost four inches in diameter, its tawny millstone grit blackened with Euston soot (in author's possession).

The Princess Victoria twice attended the exhibition in Trafalgar Square in these weeks of more active public life marked by her eighteenth birthday on May 24, when she attained her majority by Act of Parliament 'in the event of a demise of the Crown'. This year her birthday was observed as a sort of public holiday, with 'a splendid flag of pure white silk, on which was inscribed, in letters of ethereal blue, the princess's name', flying over Kensington Palace in the country air. (The date inscribed on one paw of the noble Coade-stone lion made for the river-front of the Lion Brewery on the site of the Festival Hall, and now installed at the County Hall end of Westminster Bridge, is 24 May 1837.)

In July, the Queen moved from the old red-brick palace where she had been born to 'the new Palace' where Nash's expensive recasting of Buckingham House surrounded her with colonnades and porticoes that amused a scholarly German visitor (Waagen): 'It looks as if some wicked magician had suddenly transformed some capricious stage scenery into solid reality'—a thought that might have amused George IV for whom it was intended. The Palace was to be partially masked in the Forties by an unimpressive east front (*Fig. 57*, designed by Edward Blore and executed by the firm of Thomas Cubitt) that lasted until the reign of George V. In 1837 the palace-forms of the moment stood near the other end of St James's Park.

As William IV came to the throne in 1830, an old architect's *palazzo* was rising opposite the east end of St James's Park: Soane's State Paper Office, incorporating certain features of Wren's Marlborough House on the north side of the Park. And a young man's *palazzo*, Barry's Travellers' Club, was rising nearby in Pall Mall. By 1837 Barry was planning its grander neighbour, the Reform Club, that became one of the great models of the Forties. By the Sixties, when Soane's building made way for Gilbert Scott's Foreign Office, and Wren's mansion was altered for the Prince of Wales to live in, every new office building or hotel was a palace, grand as any club.

A lowlier form of palace-model was better known to most of the population in 1837: the gin palace. Its aggrandizement had been a feature of the early Thirties, described as the onset of a disease in *Sketches by Boz*:

The primary symptoms were an inordinate love of plate-glass, and a passion for gas-lights and gilding . . . onward it has rushed to every part of town, knocking down all the old public-houses, and depositing splendid mansions, stone balustrades, rosewood fittings, immense lamps, and illuminated clocks, at the corner of every street . . . they are invariably numerous and splendid, in precise proportion to the dirt and poverty of the surrounding neighbourhood. The gin-shops in and near Drury-lane, Holborn, St Giles's, Covent Garden, and Clare-market, are the handsomest in London. There is more of filth and squalid misery near those great thoroughfares than in any part of this mighty city.

The John Kemble, or Kemble Tavern (now Kemble's Head and somewhat altered since the view in Knight's *London*), at the corner of Bow Street and Long Acre must have been one of these; its proximity to the cool Doric of Covent Garden Opera House (as rebuilt 1809) must have suggested its original giant order of pilasters. These are now truncated, but its upper portions still bear the sort of mongrel enrichments attending what has sometimes been called the Fancy Style. The original effect of the giant gas lamps hanging outside these 'corner houses'—one, about 1838–40, is said to have had a lamp ten feet high with seventy gas-jets in it—shining out into the fog and mud of a dark street in a poor neighbourhood can be imagined. Cruikshank drew them at Seven Dials. What a difference between the warm brightness inside and dank walls, ageing floorboards and smelly draughts at home where the water wasn't drinkable anyway.

In better-off neighbourhoods the greenish-white light of gas street lamps suited cream-painted stucco house fronts, even brownish or yellowish brick fronts, in the first half of the century, better than it suited red-brick and terracotta fronts later on. Interiors of many private houses lighted by candles or oil lamps changed to gas after about 1840, until 'the electric light' began to appear in the Eighties and Nineties. Evening dress of shiny materials such as satins and lamé, elaborate metal ornaments and jewellery, that would seem gaudy under brighter light, glistened and glimmered under the gas lamps; and perhaps it mattered less that women did less with their faces.

'Street architecture' was to be a favourite term of Victorian architectural critics for what amounted to a string of commercial façades; our eyes see it as street scenery. John Claudius Loudon said in 1834, on founding his short-lived *Architectural Magazine*, that the 'Street Architecture of London does not . . . get a tithe of the attention which it ought to have from architects; which is the

9

more surprising since it is likely soon to constitute a principal part of their employment'. One architect who had been paying a good deal of attention to shops was John Buonarotti Papworth, ever since his first showroom for Rudolf Ackermann in the Strand in 1812, and his work included a gin palace on Holborn Hill completed in 1832. Barry turned his hand to designing a shop building for a tailor in Pall Mall, nearly opposite the Travellers' Club, in 1833 (demolished). Far ahead of its time—except for some French precedents—its two main storeys were ruled by vertical wall-strips sandwiching window-and-panel strips between them. A straitened version was to be the gaunt pattern of fronts in Milner Square, Islington (by Gough & Roumieu, 1841).

Architects had just organized themselves professionally when Victoria came to the throne. An Institute of British Architects was formed in 1834 and met for three years in an old house in Covent Garden, a period of prehistory culminating in the grant of a royal charter early in 1837 (another of the last acts of William IV's life). Officially (although seldom called so then in public) it became the Royal Institute of British Architects on all printed notices of its meetings, beginning with the 1837–8 session in November 1837. Securing quarters at 16 Grosvenor Street, the Institute met in that Georgian house (altered now but still standing) until the move to Conduit Street in 1859. This lively professional organization, reflecting in its history so much that happened to the fabric of London, had coalesced in that germinal pre-Victorian period sometimes ignored by Georgian and Victorian historians alike, the mid-Thirties.

Whatever architectural fashions shouldered one another on the central London street-scene over the following century, the classical entablature was to provide its deep ledges, or starlings' rests, for hordes of London birds (ornithological variety), suburban by day, that now commute inward at dusk above the outward surge of human commuters. Only a clean sweep of inner London by modern curtain-wall construction could end its nights as starling-dormitory.

In 1837, the Oxford Street shop assistant who now arrives every morning from Ealing or Hornchurch or Tooting, lived like Tittlebat Titmouse, the vulgar little hero of *Ten Thousand A-Year*, in a 'dismal back attic in one of the closest courts adjoining Oxford Street'. On a Sunday morning his clothes lay where he had flung them an hour after midnight, 'at which time he had returned from a great draper's shop in Oxford Street, where he served as a shop-man, and where he had nearly dropped asleep, after a long day's work, in the act of putting up the shutters'. The draper himself, Mr Tag-rag of Tag-rag & Co., lived in his villa called Satin Lodge at Clapham.

Textile manufacturers and wholesale or retail drapers had been next after the ironmasters to profit by the Industrial Revolution; the first factories in the world had produced cotton in Lancashire, and the first London shopkeepers to indulge in plate-glass, gas lamps, carved wood and gilding—before the publicans did—were the retail drapers. The textile wholesalers, or Manchester-ware-housemen, of the Cheapside–St Paul's area (some of whom deigned to 'break bulk' and sell retail as well) were to become merchant princes like their counterparts in Manchester and Liverpool. William Cook, who had come up from Norfolk to London in 1806 to seek his fortune, worked his way up through the drapery trade in Cheapside and in 1834 set up opposite the south porch of St Paul's, where twenty years later a warehouse *palazzo* was to be built for him. Out of it his son Francis, later first baronet, was to found the great Cook Collection of old-master paintings during the last forty years of Victoria's reign, and after, partly in a mansion on Richmond Hill, partly in a palace-villa in Portugal. And there was George Moore from Cumberland who arrived in 1825 to seek his fortune, and became a partner in a great lace warehouse in Bow Churchyard with a factory at Nottingham; an active philanthropist in his lifetime, he was to leave in 1876 so many charitable bequests that his will has been cited as an extreme example of the 'scatteration' philosophy of charity. For vigorous men like these, like Thomas Cubitt and many another on the brink of the new reign in 1837, London was their America, their new-found land. A process older than Dick Whittington.

To set the scene in 1837 properly, one could go on and on. (Sir Laurence Gomme had a good try at it sixty years later: *London in the Reign of Victoria*, 1898.) Old streets like Fleet Street were still lined with narrow house-size buildings (*Fig. 3*). The south side of Piccadilly, between Regent Street and St James's Street consisted of about fifty little buildings, aside from the church (as built up in the late seventeenth century, there had been fifty-five). By 1901, after a queen's reign of rebuilding and amalgamation, this stretch contained twenty buildings. Leadenhall and other streets in the City outside the path of the Great Fire still had some medieval

Fig. 3 *Numbers 46–53 Fleet Street in 1838 and in 1847*

houses, gabled affairs with overhanging storeys projecting by more than four feet. One day in November 1847, the front of 70 Leadenhall Street, occupied by a toyman, was caught by a heavily laden wagon: 'The carman, not being aware of the danger, and having a powerful team, whipped up his horses . . . when a terrific crash was heard'— the house front collapsed and knocked down a policeman. Yet in 1837 a spanking new street, Moorgate, was being completed in the City in the stuccoed classic style of Regent Street, that is, of the Twenties, as part of the improved approaches to the new London Bridge. In the West End, the complicated overlay detectable in trade directories shows, for example, that the early eighteenth-century pair of houses in New Bond Street that were to house in the 1870s the immense paintings of Gustave Doré, and today the firm of Sotheby's, accommodated in 1837 a livery stable and a perfumer to the Royal Family. Three little houses opposite, to be rebuilt in the Seventies as the greenery-yallery Grosvenor Gallery (now Aeolian Hall), were the premises of a wine and brandy merchant, a breeches maker, and a carver and gilder. And so the continual palimpsest, or compost, accumulated.

From Chelsea to the City there were seven bridges over the Thames, all Georgian. Late in 1831, as soon as New London Bridge was opened, demolition had begun on Old London Bridge, slowly, to allow surveys of the effect on the tide to be taken all the way up to Teddington; it was wholly removed by 1834, and barges that had had to be horse-drawn from Putney to Richmond were now borne from London Bridge to Richmond on one tide. The marvel of the first tunnel excavation under the river went on against all obstacles (Brunel's Thames Tunnel, 1828–43). The docks already built north of the river were, from west to east, St Katharine's, London, Limehouse, West India, East India; south of the river, Grand Surrey, Commercial (with the old Greenland Dock), and the Royal Dock Yard. 'So vast an amount of Shipping and Commerce, which belongs to the Port of London, was never previously concentrated in any single Port'—McCulloch, *Dictionary of Commerce*, quoted

Fig. 4 *Pre-Victorian warehouse, Upper Thames Street (site of present Mermaid Theatre)*

approvingly by James Elmes as Surveyor to the Port in his *Scientific, Historical, and Commercial Survey of the Harbour and Port of London*, 1838. Seven-storey warehouses stood along both sides of the river. One at Puddle Dock stood above the others with its gabled roof (*Fig. 4*); after destruction in the last war, it provided a shell for the present Mermaid Theatre, still with the original Doric-columned entrance. Such warehouse height (before lifts worked by little steam-engines appeared in the Fifties) was made possible by various hoists for goods, and 'jigger-ropes' for fire-escapes for the warehousemen. This was probably the greatest height attained by brick walls until Queen Anne's Mansions was begun in the Seventies.

The counting-houses and warehouses concentrated in the City, with the forest of masts on its doorstep, constituted the emporium of the world. And just beginning to nibble at the outskirts of the metropolis were railways, heading towards Southwark, Vauxhall, Euston, and Paddington (twelve enabling acts for the London area had been passed under William IV). Monumental railway termini, future 'cathedrals of the nineteenth century', were yet to come.

The interior of London's elder cathedral, St Paul's, was a dusty marble catafalque in 1837, where one paid to enter—a tip to the verger for a seat during a service, or a series of fees to view different portions of the church. Westminster Abbey's brown gloom was a dusty catafalque too. Both kept their freezing naves for state occa-sions only, and screened their services within the choir. Yet popular antiquarianism was about to raise its head, handbooks and tours of the 'Architecture, Sculpture, Tombs, and Decoration' of the Abbey were shortly to be arranged, with vergers leading visitors around 'at a railway pace'. This medievalist enthusiasm was perhaps partly stimulated by excitement over the Coronation, partly by populariza-tion of the Gothic Revival even by designers of shopfronts (such as 22 Gerrard Street, elaborately traceried for an engraver's shop in the Thirties, long since disappeared).

Churches were still being built or rebuilt in central London: St Peter Saffron Hill (by Barry, meagre Perpendicular, consecrated 1832; demolished) to minister to the overcrowded 'depraved classes' in the parish of St Andrew, Holborn; St Dunstan-in-the-West (by John Shaw, consecrated 1833), rebuilt in line with frontages either side where the old church had jutted into the traffic, still pricking the skyline with its open-lanterned tower near the bend in Fleet Street; and Trinity Church (by John Shaw, Anglo-Norman, con-secrated 1838; demolished) on a triangular plot behind Fleet Street near Gough Square, built to relieve the overcrowded parish of St Bride's. The forest of steeples to be seen from the Thames were, Citywards, still Wren's, and the three defining the Strand, still Gibbs's. Further afield, thin Gothic spires had risen, such as those of Lewis Vulliamy at Bloomsbury (Woburn Square, demolished) and Highgate, contemporary with John Shaw's churches. The pure wave of Christian Hellenism of the Twenties was spent.

With hospitals the pattern of outer forms had been similar, the most recent in London being St George's at Hyde Park Corner, of the Twenties (by William Wilkins), vaguely Greek, and the West-minster, vaguely Tudor (by W. and C. F. Inwood, 1832–3; demo-lished), opposite the Abbey, where a car-park now sits. In 1837 the most recent theatre built in London was the St James's (demolished), in which the witty theatre architect Samuel Beazley improved on the Fancy Style of gin palace and draper's shop. The firework displays at Vauxhall Gardens were fancier than any mere building style.

London's longest-running continuous architectural performance on a large scale before the rebuilding of the Houses of Parliament was still going on in Bloomsbury—Sir Robert Smirke's British Museum. The seventeenth-century building was still there, with its picturesque gate-lodge, while building went on behind them. It was not generally known in 1837 what the new front would look like.

On the eve of the illustrated periodical explosion, careful depiction of London's street scenery was in the hands of skilled view-makers like Thomas Hosmer Shepherd, sharp-eyed toward actual buildings, inserting a little decorous life around the edges, while George Cruikshank's comic views were the other way round. We go to writers for a stronger sense of life hurtling through the London of 1837: *Oliver Twist* on Smithfield Market, Tennyson's lines later incorporated in *Maud*, and the famous paragraphs in *Nicholas Nickleby*. These are often quoted, for good reason. For a sense of London then, as sensed by two abnormally fine-strung sensibilities, run them together, thus:

It was market-morning. The ground was covered, nearly ankle-deep, with filth and mire; a thick steam, perpetually rising from the reeking bodies of the cattle, and mingling with the fog, which seemed to rest upon the chimney-tops, hung heavily above . . . the whistling of drovers, the barking of dogs, the bellowing and plunging of oxen, the bleating of sheep, the grunting and squeak-ing of pigs, the cries of hawkers, the shouts, oaths, and quarrelling on all sides; the ringing of bells and roar of voices, that issued from every public-house; the crowding, pushing, driving, beating, whooping, and yelling; the hideous and discordant din that resounded from every corner of the market; and the unwashed, unshaven, squalid, and dirty figures constantly running to and fro, and bursting in and out of the throng; rendered it a stunning and bewildering scene, which quite confounded the senses.

> When all my spirit reels
> At the shouts, the leagues of lights,
> And the roaring of the wheels. . . .

They rattled on through the noisy, bustling, crowded streets of London, now displaying long double rows of brightly-burning lamps, dotted here and there with the chemists' glaring lights, and illuminated besides with the brilliant flood that streamed from the windows of the shops. . . . Streams of people apparently without end poured on and on, jostling each other in the crowd and hurrying forward, scarcely seeming to notice the riches that surrounded them on every side; while vehicles of all shapes and makes, mingled up together in one moving mass like running water, lent their ceaseless roar to swell the noise and tumult.

. . . The rags of the squalid ballad-singer fluttered in the rich light that showed the goldsmith's treasures; pale and pinched-up faces hovered about the windows where was tempting food; hungry eyes wandered over the profusion guarded by one thin sheet of brittle glass—an iron wall to them; half-naked shivering figures stopped to gaze at Chinese shawls and golden stuffs of India. There was a christening party at the largest coffin-maker's, and a funeral hatchment had stopped some great improvements in the bravest mansion. Life and death went hand in hand; wealth and poverty stood side by side; repletion and starvation laid them down together.

London crowds could be decorous. When the Queen was about to make her first state visit to the City in November 1837, the pavements along her route were 'densely studded by a numerous, respectable, and anxious body' of her subjects; in the Strand, where people still lived, house fronts were hung with bright-coloured cloths and green boughs. And for the Coronation procession (from the Palace by way of Hyde Park Corner, Piccadilly, St James's Street, Pall Mall, Charing Cross and Whitehall to the Abbey), 'habitations in the line of march cast forth their occupants to the balconies or the house-tops . . . windows were lifted out of their frames, and the asylum of private life . . . made accessible to the gaze of the entire world'; 'the suburbs seemed to have emptied themselves of all their residents at once', the streets were 'paved with heads', so that 'it seemed as if the entire people—no longer an abstraction or a phrase—but the *nation*,—all ages, sexes, conditions, trades, arts, and professions—embodied visibly into one harmonious and exalted whole'; the peaceable behaviour of hundreds of thousands of people 'in the middle and lower ranks of life' drew the admiration of all foreigners present (*Annual Register*). And the journalistic catch-phrase for London itself was 'not a city but a nation'.

In that Coronation June of 1838, London was full of tourists (four hundred thousand visitors added to London's million and a half, reported the Chancellor of the Exchequer), with more distinguished visitors than in any year since the 'summer of sovereigns' in 1814. It was a foretaste of the shoals of sightseers to arrive for the Exhibitions of 1851 and 1862—in fact, a Victorian revival of the medieval pilgrim phenomenon, streaming like salmon up the hills of Rome and over the Downs to Canterbury. It was for that crowd of strangers—provincials and foreigners—in Coronation summer that the astute young publisher John Tallis started his weekly *Street Views* of the thoroughfares of the metropolis, complete with simple maps and potted facts in the best guidebook tradition. The word 'sightseeing' was not yet invented, but London visitors had been at it for centuries. Perhaps pride in London's sights was reborn in 1837.

In 1837 Darwin, Gladstone, and Tennyson were 28, and Dickens was 25; Ruskin and Bazalgette, George Eliot and Frith, like the new Queen, were 18; in April, Constable died and Swinburne was born; and children due to reach the age of 63 in the year of the Queen's death were only a flash in their parents' eyes. In 1837, Napoleon was nearer in popular memory than Hitler is to us. Men and women in their fifties, hearing Victoria's accession proclaimed at St James's, Temple Bar or the Royal Exchange on that summer's day, could recall the alarms of the French Revolution.

A generation of architects in their fifties in 1837, who had 'improved' London in the 1820s, themselves remained in a sense Georgians however long they lived into the new reign (J. B. Papworth, 1775–1847; Sir Robert Smirke, 1781–1867). And there was in 1837 a generation in its thirties and early forties who had started

17

C

practice in the 1820s and whose first successes came in the 1830s—
William IV men all their lives, ready for great things, not entirely
Georgians nor utterly Victorians (Sir Charles Barry, 1795–1860;
Sir William Tite, 1798–1873). Early Victorian London was formed
by Late Georgians and William IV men. Even Sir George Gilbert
Scott (1811–78)—who crowned his career, and the Prince Consort,
with that Victorian reliquary the Albert Memorial—had a Georgian
apprenticeship.

If the relevant year for a man's awareness of his world was his
twenty-first, it was the generation come of age after 1840—to whom
Waterloo was parents' talk, not a shiver at shouts in the street—
who were the first Victorians entire (George Edmund Street,
1824–81; William Burges, 1827–81). These and the ones who
came of age with the Crystal Palace (E. M. Barry, 1830–80;
Alfred Waterhouse, 1830–1905) shaped Mid-Victorian London and,
in the case of Waterhouse, became one sort of Late Victorian; while
others in that second wave, directly or indirectly, formed a good deal
of Late Victorian London (R. Norman Shaw, 1831–1912; Philip
Webb, 1831–1915). Still later Victorian Londoners, not yet born in
1837, came of age after 1860 (Thomas Collcutt, 1840–1924; C.
Harrison Townsend, 1851–1928).

It appeared on 20 June 1837 that the Queen herself, like the
Modern Babylon, might go on and on and on.

CHAPTER TWO

The Forties:
Daguerreotype Panorama

On Friday, 13 May 1842, a young man about to launch a new weekly publication put 200 men on the streets of London carrying signs proclaiming 'ILLUSTRATED LONDON NEWS 30 ENGRAVINGS PRICE 6*d*'. Next day it came out and weekly illustrated journalism was here to stay. With improved presses and new techniques of using engraved wood blocks with printer's type, the 'wonderful march of periodical literature' was just then being 'given an impetus and a rapidity almost coequal with the gigantic power of steam' (opening address, *ILN*, 14 May 1842). Herbert Ingram had foreseen that the regular use of illustrations would sell a weekly paper; at first he had thought of confining it to crime reports, but was then persuaded that rising new middle-class Londoners were ready to read, not too ponderously, about politics, shipwrecks, diplomacy, fashions, new buildings *and* murders, as well as 'the pleasures of the people' and especially of the aristocracy, 'the complexion of their grandeur, and the circumstance of all their pomp!' Volume One ended with *Marriages and mortality in high life in 1842*, and a hymn to London, *The city of the world*, for voice and pianoforte. Never mind that not one of the thirty-two illustrations in that first issue, John Gilbert the artist said later, was from life. The *Illustrated London News* soon made up for it by going to immense trouble to take a likeness of London itself.

This likeness was taken by daguerreotype from the top of the Duke of York's Column in Waterloo Place. The resulting pair of views, panoramic sweeps northward and southward, were printed as one folding supplement and given with the first issue of 1843 (see details on endpapers). Converting the original plates into the final published views took months; the whole idea must have been

19

thought up soon after the paper was founded. The process was described with much relish for technical difficulties overcome. Free access to the Column and leave to fix apparatus at the top having been obtained, M. Claudet took the view on a great number of small silver plates which had to be copied (drawn presumably) and arranged in position, with any gaps filled in by an artist working many days at the top of the Column. Then this view was drawn on wood for engraving, more than sixty boxwood blocks having been joined together to make one surface; the engraving was super-intended by Ebenezer Landells with the assistance of eighteen other engravers, specialists in buildings, foliage, tints etc., working for two months 'night and day'. Then, as such a large piece of wood was likely to warp and split with the heat and moisture of the printing machine, the engraving was stereotyped, mounted as separate plates on smaller blocks, inspected and retouched, and finally passed to the steam press to portray 'London, mighty London!'

The daguerreotype panorama was, inevitably, the still view of the still-photographer, full of proud buildings and vast distances but suggesting little of the 'stirring multitude' or that 'great crush and crash of carts and wains' Disraeli heard in *Tancred* (1847), purged of the 'driving, hurrying, marrying, burying' atmosphere Tennyson felt and added later to the excitable strain of *Maud*. 'London is not an abstraction, a mere city of streets and dwellings,' said the editor of the *Builder* (then Alfred Bartholomew) in 1843, 'London is two millions of human beings.' We can fill out the pano-rama with recollections such as those of a young Scot, David Masson (later editor of *Macmillan's Magazine*), in 1843 newly arrived in London by boat from Aberdeen and taking his first cab ride from the dock at Wapping to Marylebone: 'The drive of four or five miles seemed interminable. Streets, streets, streets, at first chokingly narrow and monotonously alike, but gradually broader and more various; and in every street shops and their signboards, shops and their signboards, till one grew dizzy with looking out! Such an impression of vastness and populousness one had never received before . . . what an enormous aggregate of wakeful humanity.' Masson's memories of his introduction to London that summer of 1843 also recalled his first sensation while sitting on a bench in Green Park one evening of a phenomenon he always there-after thought of as 'the Roar of Piccadilly':

> . . . ceaselessly and not intermittently, there comes a roar or boom, as if all the noises of all the wheels of all the carriages in creation

were mingled and ground together into one subdued, hoarse, moaning hum, not unpleasing, but melancholy and mystical. . . . A similar roar . . . is audible on top of St Paul's; but that vertical or ascending roar . . . may be distinguished . . . from the horizontal roar. . . . All day, and, I believe, all night, it goes on. . . . Melancholy I have called it; but that may depend on the mood of the listener . . . that roar . . . continuous in his ear as if a sea-shell were held close to it, and telling of the pitiless immensity of life and motion.

Even inside St Paul's, there was a 'strange and solemn noise within the dome, when the roar of the surrounding tumult is gathered and magnified' (*Builder*, 29 August 1857). Even in the Seventies, 'in the middle of Regent's Park or Hyde Park, one heard the roar of the traffic all round in a ring of tremendous sound' (Stephen Coleridge, looking back in 1913). Dickens converted the London Sound into an operatic *continuo* accompanying the murder of Mr Tulkinghorn: 'every noise is merged, this moonlight night, into a distant ringing hum, as if the city were a vast glass, vibrating.'

Prosaically, the roar of the streets was partly a matter of untyred wheels (rubber tyres only came slowly into use after about 1870), partly a matter of heavy wagons without springs and the hooves of many horses, and partly a matter of paving materials. These last were of great municipal concern as traffic intensified in weight and numbers, becoming continuous 'like one great dragon' (*Bleak House*). In 1839, a series of experimental street-pavements were laid down in Oxford Street. Twelve portions of the 500-foot stretch from Tottenham Court Road to what is now Soho Street were placed at the disposal of various companies to try out the virtues of different treatments with wood, granite, asphalt or bitumen. Although wood thereafter became the preferred street-paving, it was very slippery in wet weather and methods of grooving its surface and laying the grain diagonally or transversely were much debated; in 1843 a wood paving near the Mansion House was 'the subject of much animadversion and bickering, and many votes' (*Companion to the British Almanac for 1844*). There was solid-stone road surface in Fleet Street, the broken-stone variety in Regent's Street and, with some asphalt, in Whitehall; Piccadilly from the Haymarket to St James's was paved with granite laid partly diagonally, partly transversely, from thence to Devonshire House with wood, then granite to Clarges Street, then a bit of wood paving laid diagonally, then macadamized to Half Moon Street, then more granite, and finally

21

macadamized the rest of the way to Hyde Park Corner—crazy-paving indeed. The asphalt method was first patented in 1837, and then assorted mixtures with iron or fibre or rubber were tried out. There was a school of thought that advocated the use of different materials for footpath, gutter, wheel-tracks, horsepath, and centre. Parish boundaries, often down the centre of a street, and a multiplicity of paving boards contributed to the piecemeal approach to paving the larger thoroughfares.

The need to shut a shop door before one could hear to speak inside, can have been little worse than the effect of jet aircraft in summer on present-day London conversation, yet the memories of people who were children in the carriage age suggest that the confusion of unpredictable hooves and tall wheels made traffic as frightening to pedestrians as speed makes it now. Not to mention horse-droppings and mud. Overcrowded old streets, even before railway termini began to polarize the jams, demanded new streets.

Victoria Street had been conceived in the early Thirties as a route between the old Palace of Westminster, where Parliament and the Law Courts sat, and the new Buckingham Palace, to improve the crowded approaches to these buildings and incidentally the drainage of the low-lying land between. Much of that land was covered by a huddle of ancient houses, alleys, almshouses and schools that were remnants of medieval or later foundations, neighbourhoods where Chaucer and Caxton and Milton had lived, and the rookery south-west of the Abbey, once a sanctuary for diseased poor and criminals seeking help or anonymity on the doorsteps of religious hospitals there. Further southward, the labyrinth of dirty lanes tailed off into market gardens on the alluvial ground extending to the river and the Chelsea Canal, until that ground called Pimlico was cultivated by the master builder Thomas Cubitt in the Twenties. The immediate neighbourhood of the new Victoria Street was a combination of rural slum and urban fringe for some time. An Act of 1845 placed the development of the street itself in the hands of a Westminster Improvement Commission. By 1851 an eighty-foot roadway had been carved through the 'wilderness of purlieus' (as Baedeker was to put it) from Broad Sanctuary before the Abbey to the banks of Grosvenor Basin at the head of the road to Vauxhall Bridge, that is, to the edge of what was to become the forecourt of Victoria Station. Although building along Victoria Street began in 1852, it was then to languish, an arrested development, until the Sixties.

A more central improvement was made during 1843–5 when the north side of the enclave of Leicester Square was carved open by the eastward extensions of Coventry Street into the square and of Cranbourn Street to the junction of Long Acre and St Martin's Lane. *Punch* thought this 'expedition to the interior of Leicester Square', where who knew what 'native tribes' might still abide from the 'centuries it has remained undisturbed', rendered the undertaking 'equal in importance to the exhumation of Pompeii and Herculaneum'. After circulation was improved, the Punch-and-Judy man told Henry Mayhew at the end of the Forties: 'The best pitch of all in London is Leicester-square; there's all sorts of classes, you see, passing there.' The need for these short lengths of redevelopment, as links in improved east–west communication between Piccadilly and the areas north of the Strand, had been recognized by a House of Commons Committee on Metropolitan Improvements in 1838. At the same time it was noted that traffic using the vital artery of Oxford Street, at its east end had to go round by the narrow St Giles High Street toward High Holborn to approach the City via Newgate. This and the other principal ways, besides the river, between West End and City—the Strand/Fleet Street/St Paul's Churchyard/Cheapside route and the New Road from Paddington via Islington and City Road—became more and more choked with traffic generated by the docks, the railways, and the shops. It was easier to ride to Brighton on the new railway line than to 'storm your way from Hyde Park Corner to the Surrey side of London Bridge' to catch the train (*ILN*, 1 November 1845).

So, during 1843–7, New Oxford Street was driven through another rookery even worse than the one at Westminster. This roughly lozenge-shaped territory just north-east of the church of St Giles-in-the-Fields (such fields) was bounded roughly by the High Street and Broad Street, Dyott Street and Bainbridge Street (the last now just north of the new thoroughfare). It was built up initially in the seventeenth century. By 1840, 'it was one dense mass of houses, through which curved narrow tortuous lanes, from which again diverged close courts—one great mass, as if the houses had originally been one block of stone, eaten by slugs into numberless small chambers and connecting passages' (John Timbs, *Curiosities of London*). Such districts were 'composed almost entirely of small courts, very small and very narrow, the access to them being only under gateways; in many cases . . . larger courts originally . . . built in again with houses back to back . . . occupied by an immense number of inhabitants' (James Pennethorne, architect, reporting to parliamentary committee, 1840). Perhaps there were three factors in this horrible growth: dispersed ownership among numerous landlords beginning with division of the property among three daughters of the man who bought it in 1649; its backwater position; and the efficient management of the Bedford Estate north of it, for good estate planning meant slums somewhere else. *Punch*, socially conscious in 1844, saw that the demolition of the St Giles Rookery would be 'a great boon to boots; a blessing to sensibilities, olfactory and sympathetic; and a heavy blow . . . to typhus into the bargain', yet could not help hearing 'the outcry of the unlucky rooks . . . a dismal caw. . . . "Where shall we go? . . ." And a mournful, a very mournful echo . . . answers, "Heaven only knows!" Does the Government?' The Government housed no poor. In the autumn of 1844, *Punch* imagined one of the half-demolished old streets appealing thus: 'I was dirty in my habits—my drainage far from perfect . . . but still I gave the poor the shelter of a roof. Again I say to the upstart new streets, with their nicely stuccoed faces and heavy rents—hopelessly I say it—"Go ye and do likewise"' (the old to the new Covent Garden in the 1970s?). The miserable outcasts in the path of New Oxford Street pushed on to other already overcrowded courts and alleys in nearby parishes, even as far as Lambeth. As their children uprooted by roads and railways in the Sixties were to push on to new slums on old market-garden ground at Fulham.

While New Oxford Street's floridly stuccoed faces were let to new sorts of tenants (Mudie's Library is in the next chapter), the old junction of St Giles High Street with High Holborn was being linked with Long Acre, Bow Street and the Strand by the carving through of Endell Street; but there was no Shaftesbury Avenue yet and the way to Charing Cross lay through the narrow ways of Seven Dials.

In the City in 1846, there were plans for the westward extension of Cannon Street (which ran originally between Walbrook and Abchurch Lane, taken east of that by Westcheap), to relieve the choked traffic of Cheapside by adding another opening to St Paul's Churchyard for the streams up and down Ludgate Hill and to provide direct communication with London Bridge. The demolitions involved in cutting more than a quarter of a mile of new street through alleyfuls of old houses, not counting frontage changes in the Churchyard itself, took place between the west edge of the future Cannon Street Station site and Old Change. It seems not to have occurred to anyone to remove through-traffic from St Paul's Churchyard altogether—the drapers installed so profitably around its rim would hardly have stood for it. The Dean and Chapter continued to bar through-traffic on the north side with their toll-gate, for which they were to be roundly abused for some time by would-be planners of one-way traffic all the way round the Cathedral, to help relieve 'the conflict of wains and 'buses, the laboring of horses, the retardation of trucks', in fact 'the constipated condition of traffic throughout the civic arteries of trade' (*Builder*, 2 December 1859). Queen Victoria Street, along what had been a projected alternative route for Cannon Street to Blackfriars, was to be put through in the Sixties.

Above the traffic of Hyde Park Corner in 1846, rose a colossal form pointing a gawky arm Citywards: Matthew Cotes Wyatt's equestrian statue of the Duke of Wellington, as awkwardly immobile as the same sculptor's George III in Pall Mall East was gracefully mobile. For its installation, 'this gigantic triumph of bad taste over public opinion' (*Punch*) was extracted from the sculptor's foundry in the Harrow Road, after removal of the roof, by a hoisting device under the care of Messrs Grissell & Peto and put on a carriage for its majestic progress down the Edgware Road (and *Punch* invented a list of regulations—'1. No one is to laugh'—with a cartoon of bronze horse's head seen through second-storey window, 'awful apparition' etc.). It was placed upon the Constitution Arch, which then stood opposite the Hyde Park Screen and almost in front of Apsley House, much to the distress of the arch's architect, Decimus Burton, and there it dominated the Duke's view from his front windows for the last six years of his life, and the view of all passers-by until 1883 when, to everyone's relief, it was removed to Aldershot. (The present uncolossal statue of Wellington at Hyde Park Corner, by Boehm, dates from 1888.) It appears, by the way, that Matthew Cotes Wyatt was not only a sculptor but a speculator in London property. Cubitt's biographer has discovered in various estate and insurance records that a Matthew Cotes Wyatt was not only one of the developers of Victoria Square but of Tyburnia, almost within view of his house in Harrow Road. No wonder he left a good deal of money when he died in 1862.

Meanwhile, those long-playing public performances, the erection of the British Museum (1823–47), the adornment of Trafalgar Square (1840–67) and the building of the Houses of Parliament (1837–60), went on accompanied by increasingly disparaging public comment. When the Museum's great colonnade was done at last in 1847, the seventeenth-century pavilions with their concave-curved roofs stood for a while in front of it with a picturesque air that appealed to the tastes of 1847 more than Smirke's pure Ionic columns did. It was hardly necessary to demonstrate the effect of Grecian colonnades any more, thought one bored critic who never-theless, a year later, regretted the removal of Nash's Doric colon-nades from the Regent Street Quadrant—those had the picture-squeness ('richness' was the key word) of curved lines disappearing round the bend. But the Quadrant colonnades had shaded shop windows and sheltered undesirables (let alone decent shoppers from the rain), they were in restraint of trade, so they went. And elegant fluted sixteen-foot cast iron columns were to be had at £15 the pair. Some said a railway company bought the lot.

At Westminster in 1847, the Lords were at last able to move into their chamber, ten years after foundations were started, but work on the House of Commons was still going on at the end of the Forties. In April 1847, the two towers were ninety-foot stumps. One operation early in 1848 gratifyingly combined the antiquarian and the technological: forty stone-carvers on scaffolds sculpturing the elaborately detailed ceiling bosses on the vaults of the central hall, 'to rival any specimen of Gothic architecture in England', with gas-light laid on for their benefit 'not the least singular part of the scene'. (In December one of the recurrent experimental displays of 'the electric light' was held on the porch of the National Gallery, the brilliance of 'the mysterious fluid' giving a new drama to the old columns from Carlton House of which that porch is composed.)

The technology of scaffolds and travelling cranes was often more fascinating than the works they attended. The 'traveller' for hoisting building materials was a 'powerful engine moving on a railway' or 'tramway formed on the scaffold frame' operated, at first anyway, by a windlass worked by three men; the contractors Grissell & Peto used it on the Reform Club and the Houses of Parliament. One such 'travelling machine' heaving blocks of stone for the new Royal Exchange in 1843, and allegedly weighing about three tons, was caught in a gale of wind and 'precipitated into the street'. The implacably Roman portico of Tite's Royal Exchange (*Fig. 5*—however impure its back and sides) seemed to suit a civilization quickening with new techniques, even though this civilization was so much slower to perfect aqueducts and sewers than ancient Rome had been.

Fig. 5 *The Royal Exchange*

London was not itself always the source of new techniques which, for example in the matter of hoists and lifts, often came from Lancashire. The first movable cranes on scaffolding were said to have been perfected in Tomkinson's stone quarries near Liverpool for use on new docks and buildings there. Similarly, improvements on warehouse lifts seem to have been worked out at Manchester and Liverpool. London was the great adaptor and digester, the swallower.

Many variations on the lift were at work in London. An 'ascending room', winched up by a man operating a windlass, had been designed by the architect Decimus Burton (aged 23) for that public exhibition the Regent's Park Colosseum in 1823, and when new showmen modernized the place in 1845, the ascending room was brought up to date with (probably) a little steam-engine and (inevitably) an Elizabethan stained-glass ceiling inspired no doubt by the new Houses of Parliament. In Lombard Street some business houses used a species of hoist to lower and raise bulky ledgers to and from

27

fireproof vaults in the basement. Until 1971, a firm on St John's Hill, Wandsworth, had proudly painted on its premises 'Lift Specialists since 1850', a speciality originating as Johnson's building hoist, patented by a working builder. Spurgin's hoist on the endless-ladder or paternoster principle had been patented in 1836 and was being used for bricks by Cubitt and Grissell & Peto by 1843.

In 1843 one of the new cranes placed Nelson on his column (the figure designed by E. H. Bailey, the whole memorial by William Railton). The layout for Trafalgar Square was designed by Barry, skilled at landscaping awkward slopes, in 1840; his best contribution was the upper terrace that provided a much-needed visual sub-structure for the National Gallery, above the flat area for fountains (only one was originally intended) and the so-called Nelson Testi-monial ('opened' in October 1844 although the pedestal-faces were bare and no lions appeared for over twenty years: *Fig. 6*). Bronze from captured cannon formed the column's capital and the eventual reliefs on the pedestal (first to be installed was the Death of Nelson

Fig. 6 *Trafalgar Square in 1844*

on the south face in 1849). These with the Square's other dark
metallic elements—Charles I's statue, the National Gallery's prim
dome, various Victorian statues and lamp-posts, and finally Landseer's lions installed in 1867—stand in heraldic contrast to today's
cleaned stonework, pigeon and tourist swarms, and fountain displays still splashing into Barry's twin basins, at last supplied in our
century with fountain bowls and sculpture on an adequate scale.
The original 'pair of ugly dumbwaiters' (*Illustrated London News*),
'fishes with their mouths wide open, under a sort of card-tray'
(*Punch*), were the butts of the day when installed in 1844. Nevertheless, in 1835 Barry must have stood at the top of the bare slope
in front of the hoarding surrounding the works for the National
Gallery, thinking how the towers in his Parliament design could
fill the view down Whitehall—first one and then the other, depending where one stands, however cluttered the other end of Whitehall
was then. And again in 1836 when his winning design was displayed
with the others in the yet-unfinished National Gallery building, he
must have paused in the porch and thought of that view, and yet
again in 1840 while planning the Square layout. Early Victorian
Londoners may have complained that the finest site in Europe was
ruined when the layout was realized, but the view from the National
Gallery's front porch is one of the finest Early Victorian arrangements we have.

The Picturesque, in fact, was not dead, far from it. Victoria's
accession to the throne had coincided with an increased vogue for
scenic richness in architecture, and coincided also with the rise of
a new public and new artisans uninstructed in the subtle differences
between one classical entablature and another. Critics who had
complained that the 'faint projections' of classical mouldings
'seldom produce any effect in this climate' welcomed Barry's heavily
corniced new clubs in Pall Mall for combining 'boldness of effect
with richness of detail'. Long before Ruskin published his scorn for
Gower Street or Tennyson his elegiac lines on the 'bald street' that
was Wimpole Street, architects were condemning Late Georgian
'hole-in-the-wall' windows and commending Tite's new railway
station at Nine Elms for its freedom from 'disagreeable baldness'. A
trend, that is, from baldness to boldness. By 1840, public taste
preferred what Pooh-Bah was to call corroborative detail, if only a
set of stucco window-frames, for conferring artistic verisimilitude
upon otherwise bald and unconvincing structures, the stock-brick
London house front for example. For more complicated buildings,

29

pictorial groups of building forms from Italian town squares or countryside, or paintings thereof, were more accommodating than classical temples, since building types began to differ more according to function as life itself became more complicated.

One building type that became more common was the insurance company's head office. In 1839 C. R. Cockerell designed one for the Sun Assurance's corner site at Threadneedle Street and Bartholomew Lane (demolished 1971). It was a witty amalgam of French and Italian ideas with a ground-floor window-arch pattern much imitated for other office buildings and later in streets and streets of houses throughout the century; as professionally described at the time this was 'formed by stilting the segmental head some distance above the capitals or impost mouldings', and in 'common fashion' by the early Fifties. Years after the *Stones of Venice* was published in the Fifties, row upon row of little two-up two-down London houses had their Gothic or maybe Romanesque capitals, but neither round nor pointed arches to their windows; the flattened inverted-U type was so much easier to construct. Builders who were still doing that in the Nineties knew little of Ruskin and nothing of Cockerell.

A new building type of the Twenties that flourished in the Forties was the club, men's, needless to say. Barry's Reform Club in Pall Mall (first designs 1837, modified 1838, building completed 1840) was acclaimed for its 'grandeur and gusto'—gusto then could mean either taste or zest—and for its cinquecento Roman exterior, although its grand interior courtyard was in the English Palladian tradition except for its elaborate skylighting. Barry was a prime eclectic, selecting and combining from the great Renaissance ragbag. Another way of being an eclectic was to pick one building and improvise on that, as George Basevi and Sydney Smirke picked Sansovino's Library at Venice when they designed the Carlton Club next door to the Reform Club in 1844, having already produced the Conservative Club in St James's Street in a mixed-classical manner (*Fig. 7*). Such club-palaces became types for lesser palaces far from Pall Mall to imitate, suiting a new crew of clients and architects less well-read in the old intellectual rules of classical proportion.

A more vertical forerunner of blocks of flats had been designed in 1838, Club Chambers (at No. 15 Regent Street, now Cunard Line offices) by Decimus Burton, borrowing from Renaissance shop-minded palace designers the device of a low mezzanine storey tucked between ground and first, a pattern already prevalent in Regent Street and to be used in Victoria Street. Each floor was

Fig. 7 *Conservative Club, St James's, in 1844*

divided off into rooms about fifteen feet square, each with a single
window, and left to be fitted up by those who rented them; there
were seventy-seven of these 'bed-sitters', though two or more could
be let together, and the ground floor at first had refreshment and
reading rooms for the clubless. In 1850, directories listed sixty-two
esquires there. By 1880, this was the Junior Army & Navy Stores.
In the Forties the building of 'chambers', high-class lodging houses
for single men not connected with the old Inns of Court and unable
to obtain the few club bedrooms provided (for example, by Barry on
the top floor of the Reform Club), was a trend of the times: *Punch*
(1843) on Mr and Mrs Spangle Lacquer, ancestors of Dickens's

31

Veneerings, 'young Mr Lacquer haunts the thoroughfares of the West-End, and calls his lodgings chambers'; *Punch* (1847) on the Rising Generation, child telling his Governor, 'I must have Chambers'. It sounded so professional.

In the late Forties, London clubs—more and more homes-from-home whether home was a nearby lodging, a five-storey terrace house on a new square, or a villa in the suburbs—became so elaborate inside (for example, the Conservative Club and the Army and Navy Club) that Thackeray's account of the blundering splendours of the Sarcophagus was not far out:

> The great library is Elizabethan; the small library is pointed Gothic; the dining room is severe Doric; the strangers' room has an Egyptian look; the drawing rooms are Louis Quatorze . . . the *cortile*, or hall, is Morisco-Italian. It is all over marble, maplewood, looking-glasses, arabesques, ormolu, and scagliola. Scrolls, ciphers, dragons, Cupids, polyanthuses, and other flowers writhe up the walls in every kind of cornucopiosity.
>
> (Snobs of England series in *Punch*, 1847)

But more appealing than marble or looking-glasses was club cooking. Alexis Soyer's success at the Reform Club inspired other club chefs, and may have indirectly caused home cooking to improve in self-defence. Cookery books proliferated; Mrs Beeton's was not yet, but there was Francatelli's *The Modern Cook*, first issued in 1846 and reaching a twenty-eighth edition forty years later (by Charles Elmé Francatelli, chief cook to the Queen in 1841, later of the St James's Restaurant).

Out of the other end of the cornucopia of the Forties emerged new model lodging houses for the poor—model in the sense of testing and showing what could be done. Inspired by Edwin Chadwick's report of 1842, *Inquiry into the Sanitary Conditions of the Labouring Population of Great Britain* (reporting to the Home Department as secretary of the Poor Law Commissioners' investigating committee), two groups of private individuals were formed: the Metropolitan Association for Improving the Dwellings of the Industrious Classes in 1843, and the Society for Improving the Conditions of the Labouring Classes in 1844. Henry Roberts, architect of Fishmongers Hall in the previous decade, was Honorary Architect to the second society. One of the best surviving 'models' from this period was begun to his design in 1849 and opened in 1850, a five-storey block of what we call flats for forty-eight families, the Model Houses for Families in Streatham Street near New

Oxford Street on the former northern border of the old St Giles Rookery. Each household, approached from open galleries, was given a lobby, living room (with cupboard for extra bed), two bedrooms, and scullery with water-closet off it. Because of the still human scale, this was and is a very bearable building, unlike larger versions then to come. When Roberts shortly after designed a four-family unit for display near the Great Exhibition in Hyde Park, with certain structural improvements, each water-closet was still approached through the scullery. This quadruple model still stands, somewhat altered, in Kennington Park.

In the Forties, the 'Removed Poor', as such displaced persons came to be called, were driven out of their slums by new central streets much more than they were by new, not yet so central railways. The railway mania of the mid-Forties tried to cover the whole country with new lines, and filled London inns and hotels with witnesses panting to testify before parliamentary committees in aid of each new speculation's Private Bill. The rush to deposit railway plans at the Board of Trade was only slightly impeded by that building's jungle of scaffolds, as Barry brought Soane's calm façade up to date by introducing 'a certain degree of flutter' with an ornate entablature breaking in and out above the columns. But central London was still almost free of railway lines: north of the New Road were the Euston Square terminus (with a splendid new hall behind the giant gateway and, further eastward, a temporary station just north-west of the present King's Cross site; south of the river were London Bridge Station, the Bricklayers' Arms Station off the Old Kent Road, and the first Waterloo Road terminus for the line extended from Nine Elms; on the edges of the City were termini at Shoreditch (Bishopsgate) and, most central of the lot, Fenchurch Street, where the Blackwall line came in across the Minories; and there were plans to rebuild south of an existing temporary station at Paddington.

If public works dragged on expensively, railway viaducts seemed to spring into existence by magic. A certain skew arch, wider at one end than the other and so 'of very difficult build', was begun, pointed, dressed and finished 'in the almost incredible short time of *forty-five hours*!' No wonder public works seemed to need 'a tithe of the practicality exhibited by the Committee of a Railway Company'.

The commuter was already in being. In quiet chop-houses off Lombard Street, 'merchants whose autographs to a cheque would

33

D

load the bearer with gold, lunch here on their humble chop or steak
—gentlemen worth thousands—who turn up their cuffs and peel
their own potatoes', and at the day's end 'hurry off by the trains, or
omnibuses, or steamers to their snug suburban residences to dinner'
(*ILN*, 28 April 1849); 'back to their families and the fillet of veal'
(Thackeray in *Punch*, 27 September 1845). Suburbs were already
something to celebrate, pleasanter it was thought than those around
other cities from the greater contrast between the dense central
mass of men, buildings and steaming streets and the 'pure elastic
breath of Highgate-hill' (*ILN*, 18 February 1843). The result was
a vast 'villa district' tenanted by women all day while men were
'absent in enormous, smoking London' (Thackeray again). If a
man could not afford to 'bowl to town . . . in his light dog-cart and
fast mare', he could be seen 'amidst a host of his stockbroking
brothers, crowding the top of an omnibus—something after the
sitting fashion of a batch of undertaker's men going to a country job'
(back to back on the curved roof, before the knifeboard bus was
invented in 1851; *ILN*, 8 November 1845). The stockbroker belt
was said to be especially Clapham–Kennington–Brixton–Wandsworth, that is, communities ranged along ancient roads that ran
north-easterly to the City. White-collar suburbs, long before the
Pooters, were grafted on to old settlements whose only satellite
elements had been country houses—a very different thing. All
transport in the Forties was too expensive for really poor people;
labourers other than highly skilled artisans lived within walking
distance of work. That meant catastrophic upheaval for casual
labourers driven out of their homes by what one might call rookery-
clearance-without-responsibility—the crossing-sweeper, the holder
of horses' heads, the man with a regular pitch of some sort, who
managed to make a bit of a living only by living almost on top of it.
Mayhew's street folk were creatures of the Forties. And not only
the casuals, but anyone working at a trade or craft for the long
hours then expected had little time for long walks. Yet many City
workers of the Forties walked there from Peckham or Camberwell.

While the employers departed from cramped dwellings near their
counting-houses for (sometimes equally cramped) villas, sixty-eight
City churches in the ancient square mile went on holding services
for smaller and smaller congregations. Dickens sniffed the air of
these churches where 'rot and mildew and dead citizens formed the
uppermost scent, while, infused into it in a dreamy way not at all
displeasing, was the staple character of the neighbourhood'. Here

was the world emporium giving off its flavours: 'From Rood-lane to Tower-street . . . there was often a subtle flavour of wine; sometimes, of tea. One church near Mincing-lane smelt like a druggist's drawer. Behind the Monument the service had a flavour of damaged oranges, which, a little further down towards the river, tempered into herrings, and gradually toned into a cosmopolitan blast of fish.' Billingsgate still smacks of its trade, but no longer can one catch 'a dry whiff of wheat' near the former Corn Exchange in Mark Lane, though there is a sumptuous whiff of fur near St James Garlickhythe —as in one church where Dickens noted 'no speciality of atmosphere, until the organ shook a perfume of hides all over us from some adjacent warehouse' ('City of London Churches', first published in *All the Year Round* in 1860, though the decay of dead citizens was dispersed after the Metropolitan Interments Act of 1850). Sewery savours of the river hung about even in winter: visitors to the Great Exhibition were informed in one of the more honest tourist handbooks that London fog not only had its peculiar colour (from yellowish coal-smoke poured out of every chimney into the dense river-basin mists) it had a 'peculiar odour . . . not yet satisfactorily explained' but thought to have some mysterious connection with 'the sanitary state of the metropolis', or with some strange sulphurous mixture in the London clay. That is, fogs smelt of bad drains and few live citizens can have been wholly well, in or out of church.

In the Temple Church, while its restoration by a series of architects was going on in 1841, one bit of influential antiquarianism was operating in the matter of encaustic tiles. In January, with a view to finding suitable models for replacing the Georgian black-and-white pavement, the antiquarian Lewis Cottingham went to investigate the long-hidden floor tiles of the Westminster Abbey Chapter House, by taking up a floor board here and there where storage of official records allowed (the Chapter House being then degraded to store-house until a Public Record Office should be built). He found some of the wealth of designs on that wonderful floor for Minton & Co. to copy for the Temple Church. Colour-printers produced book illustrations of them, simple ones in terracotta-coloured chromolithography published right away in 1842 by John Gough Nichols, and elaborate colour plates published later by Henry Shaw. These Chapter House tile motifs, among many from other medieval sources, seem to have become one of Minton's (and other firms') regular lines, often combined in the Forties and later with 'Pompeiian' or 'Moorish' motifs. And so, on many a London doorstep or front path or hall floor for the rest of the century (quite aside from more elaborate ecclesiastical use), reproductions of medieval tiles in buff on red were set among the lozenges and triangles and frets, where they are not now recognized as souvenirs of the revived medievalism of the 1840s. Pugin's designs for Minton, not only on the floors of Parliament but in the houses and churches Pugin decorated, must have been the most fertile pattern-sources of all.

As for London's new churches in the Forties, the new periodical editors were quick to publish them as 'morsels of *pictorial news*' (*ILN*, 21 January 1843, their italic, predicting rightly that 'future historians of London will seek our columns for original views of churches now new'); at the moment that was printed, fourteen Church of England churches were said to be rising in the Metropolis. One was St Giles, Camberwell, rebuilt after a fire to the design of Scott & Moffatt (soon to go their separate ways). On the building committee sat Ruskin, aged 25, deeply concerned in advising on designs for the stained glass, especially for the east window, and sending detailed suggestions for small-scale medallions from a visit to Chartres in May 1844 (*Fig. 8*). Still a commanding-looking 'Early English' building with its tall spire, though mean streets close in around it just east of Camberwell Green, St Giles looks like the work of a powerful parson. Gilbert Scott, no weakling himself, described the incumbent as 'the most masterly brain at coping with a turbulent parish vestry I ever saw . . . a man whose very look would almost make one tremble'. Powerful parsons then affected London's skyline as much as masterful merchants did. 'Throwing money in the air', Noncomformists called it. Yet they were coming to it; for example, Bloomsbury Chapel (now Bloomsbury Central Baptist Church), given by Samuel Morton Peto the contractor and built to the design of John Gibson on part of the rescued rookery site just off New Oxford Street, was to have two spires, partly because the commissioners for the new street would only allow such use of the site if it looked properly ecclesiastical.

The new Anglican churches of the Forties looked very English, as those compiled out of Greek details in the Twenties did not. Even Wren's churches—for which there was a returning taste among some architects, and always pride among Londoners—were honorary English. But Gothic Revival architects now began to compile details out of sketches-on-the-spot of medieval parish churches and cathedrals, so far, until the end of the Forties, mostly in England.

Fig. 8 *St Giles, Camberwell*

Not only did the young clerk, the servant girl, the carpenter's apprentice, the rising new doctor or brewer or seamstress come up to London from the country to establish themselves, the pinnacles, the piscinas, the pulpits, the towers of their local village or county town churches came too, industriously recorded in the travelling sketchbooks of countless young architects and earnest members of the Ecclesiological Society. The new churches rising to minister to the new London population were the fruit of earnest country rambles, singly or in groups, by these men with sketchbooks forti- fied by published books garnering sketches compiled by the indust- rious John Britton or composed by the fertilizing genius of Pugin. Pugin's Roman Catholic church (later cathedral) of 1841–8 built of stock brick in Southwark—where Cardinal Wiseman was to be enthroned in 1850—owed something to the old church of Austin Friars in the City, something to Lincoln Cathedral. In the summer of 1847, the overturning of a dog-cart on an 'architectural scamper' in Norfolk precipitated into the road the architect to the Dean and Chapter of Norwich Cathedral (Anthony Salvin), the chief instigator of the newly formed Architectural Association (Robert Kerr), and the rather new editor of the fairly new weekly journal the *Builder* (George Godwin), all apparently with London churches on the drawing-board at home at the time (Salvin's in Uxbridge Road, Hammersmith; Kerr's in Trafalgar Road, Greenwich; and Godwin's St Mary Boltons, Kensington—neighbourhood churches of light- toned stonework, that may or may not look like anything in Norfolk, but designed and consecrated with enthusiasm).

A Londoner born in Lincolnshire, carriage-driving or hod- carrying in the City Road in 1848, might have felt at home at the sight of the new tall tower of Gilbert Scott's St Matthew (demolished after war-damage), with its spire and four stout pinnacles said to have been modelled on a famous Early English spire in fenland Lincolnshire (Long Sutton). The younger architect George Edmund Street was working in Scott's office when St Matthew was going up in the City Road, and was to recompose such a spire more freely ten years later for his own St James-the-Less, just off Vauxhall Bridge Road, Pimlico (*Fig. 31*). Looking ahead to it for a moment, while on this matter of sources, St James's tower stands almost free of the church, as the Lincolnshire tower does; Street (by then long since practising independently) had been absorbing and sketching on the Continent too, and the resulting complicated candle-snuffer silhouette, still so distinctive on our skyline, was a sophisticated exercise of 'thinking in Gothic', neither copied nor made up out of his head. London is full of echoes from Victorian architects' sketch-books if only we could hear them—the best, like Street, were improvisers on themes like composers of music.

Church-building and church-going helped many people to bear uneasiness over the violent contrasts of society, between the sense of 'We are a rich, a powerful, an intelligent, and a religious people. . . . Our spirit rules the world' (*ILN*, 22 July 1848), and of 'some-thing radically wrong in our civilisation' (Christmas supplement, 1848, after cholera had come). There was the standing army of poverty, and there were the piles of goods in the shops ('things unknown to an age that had not a Fortnum & Mason', *ILN*, Christmas 1846).

The advertising man was coming into his own. The many hoard-ings put up around new building sites and street improvements were a field for bill-stickers. Some of their favourite spots, besides the hoarding around Trafalgar Square until late April 1844 and then around Nelson's pedestal for years, included the fence at the top of the stairs to the steamboat station at the north end of Waterloo Bridge, houses about to come down for the extension of Cranbourn Street, and the west side of St James's Street where the Conservative Club was going up—hoardings postered in aid of Guinness's Dublin Stout or So-&-So's Gout and Rheumatic Oil, not to mention the playbills. And there were the advertisements on wheels, adding to the traffic jams, carts bearing great columns plastered with inscriptions about washable wigs, carts in the shape of colossal hats, carts too bulky to go through Temple Bar. One specimen, revolving on its axis by some internal clockwork as it was drawn along, was shaped like a Gothic tomb with pinnacled niches enshrining stuffed headless figures in fashionable dresses.

Drapers' shops were among the most competitive in their own design, and only the gin palaces could equal their plate-glass and gas jets. Because the gaudiest shop-window lighting of the early Forties soiled goods on display with the 'products of combustion', lamps were fixed outside the windows with reflectors inside. A Ludgate Hill shopkeeper was one of the first to cover his walls and ceiling entirely with looking-glass to reflect his 'rich cut-glass chandeliers' (probably Jones at No. 5, Cut Glass and Lustre Manu-facturers to the Royal Family, Tallis *Street Views* for 1838 and 1847). Another on Ludgate Hill was said to be the first to carry up his display windows through the first floor, a 'chasm effect' deplored by purists, and made possible by the new plate-glass sizes available (probably Harvey at No. 9, Family Linen Warehouse and Silk Mercer, Tallis *Street View*, 1847).

The elegance of Oxford Street shops was thought to be more 'correct' than these, that of Regent Street more brilliant. Even chemists' shops, once distinguished only by 'large red, and green, and yellow bottles, shedding a ghastly light on the passer-by', now displayed through their new plate-glass windows not only 'doctors' stuff' but lozenges, perfumery, soda water and powders. Produce requiring fresh air was sold in the old way; butchers and green-grocers still kept their open-fronted shops. But the grocer, in smarter neighbourhoods anyway, had advanced with plate-glass and gas lamps. Bazaars, forerunners of department stores, were established in Soho Square (north end of west side), at the Pantheon in Oxford Street, altered with a gallery in the Continental manner, and in Baker Street.

Evidence of shifts in the uses of central London neighbourhoods turns up in trade directories, if for instance one compares a directory of the late Forties with one of the late Thirties. Hungerford Market was a retail, not a wholesale, cluster built in the early Thirties to the design of Charles Fowler, at several levels descending to the river on the future site of Charing Cross Railway Station. To roof the so-called Lower Area, Fowler in 1835 invented a set of pioneering cast iron butterfly roofs that tipped rainwater down their pipelike column supports. This Lower Area went on being a slab for fish-mongers, thick with river fog in winter, thick with river smells in summer. But the Great Hall like a Roman basilica on the upper level, occupied at first entirely by fruiterers, poulterers and a few butchers, had by the late Forties a diverse lot of shopkeepers—even artisans selling not goods but services—although or because by then access to the new Hungerford footbridge went through the upper level of the market. The Roman hall was thought to 'afford a better idea to those who have not seen the originals, than anything else in London'; the prevailing atmosphere was likelier that of the homely chandler's shop near the Strand end, where Mr Peggotty found an upstairs lodging with a 'miscellaneous taste of tea, coffee, butter, bacon, cheese, new loaves, firewood, candles, and walnut ketchup, con-tinually ascending from the shop'. One of the boys working on the Market building site in the early Thirties is said to have been young Gilbert Scott, training briefly under the contractors Grissell & Peto.

Between Hungerford Market and Northumberland House,

Craven Street with its stock-brick eighteenth-century houses ran down (as still) from the Strand, ending then at a coal-wharf on the muddy riverbank. Directories for the forty-odd houses in 1837 included ten solicitors and one lodging house keeper, or, as one of the solicitors, the versifier James Smith, put it at the time:

> In Craven Street, Strand, ten attorneys find place,
> And ten dark coal-barges are moored at its base;
> Fly, Honesty, fly! seek some safer retreat,
> For there's craft in the river, and craft in the street.

By 1849 there were five solicitors and fifteen lodging house keepers. Not that lawyers in London diminished, quite the contrary, but the tone of that neighbourhood went down, except perhaps at the Strand end, as the summer stench of the river increasingly rose up. Journalists in 1847 bluntly called the Thames 'a sewer with a tide in it', as they commented on the filthy state of this very riverbank where one of central London's sewers discharged into the river at the foot of Northumberland Street—next to the bottom of the Duke of Northumberland's still-existing garden—opposite the Lambeth Waterworks' intake on the south bank. In the old hive of the Law, the Inner and Middle Temple held its collective nose in summer; in winter, as in *Bleak House*, the raw afternoon was rawest, the dense fog densest, the muddy streets muddiest 'near that leaden-headed old obstruction . . . Temple Bar'. The Temple lawyers were mainly barristers. In and around Lincoln's Inn were the conveyancers, specializing in transfers of property. Power over property (and hence over the fabric of London) operated wherever solicitors in their sets of chambers, 'like maggots in nuts' (*Bleak House*), were the investment counsellors of their day, guiding the mortgages that made property development possible, channelling the investments that produced returns 'safe as houses'. In no other society had the financing of property development on borrowed money been perfected to such an art, and most of the artists were lawyers. At least one firm of solicitors that spent much of the last century at the upper end of Craven Street still flourishes not far away today. And No. 12 Lincoln's Inn Fields, Soane's first house finally incorporated in his Museum in 1971, was preserved in solicitors, as one might put it, for more than a century.

The Yankee Herman Melville, newly arrived in November 1849 and taking a room at the foot of Craven Street, looked out over the coal barges and thought London a city of Dante, a place of the

Fig. 9 *Hungerford Bridge and coal barges in 1845*

damned in clouds of smoke. The house, No. 25, is still there, with its curved bays of 1792 now more than 500 feet from the river, but then so near the bank its windows overlooked ebb-mud or tidal heavings just above the spot where Fox Talbot (or an associate) took one of those pioneering photographs on a sunny day four years before (*Fig. 9*). The week before Melville's arrival, the *Illustrated London News* prefaced a leader on 'the blessings of coal' by imagining some foreign poet, newly arrived in London and standing on Waterloo Bridge, 'feeling upon him a slight touch of the fabulous melancholy of the place', half-seeing through the chimney-fed gloom 'the noble dome of St Paul's, and probably the glittering cross that surmounts it; but the church itself . . . invisible to his sight'; and the visitor approaching it more closely to find Wren's walls 'blackened and encrusted with a hard mixture or cement of smoke, cobwebs, and rain' (*ILN*, 3 November 1849). This said, the leader proceeded to list the blessings of coal and describe the opening of the new Coal Exchange in Lower Thames Street. The grandeur of that ceremony ('a most bloated pomp, to be sure,' said Melville of the Lord Mayor's Show the following week) had to do partly with the importance of coal among the City commodity exchanges then, partly with the outgoing Lord Mayor's membership of the Coal Factors' Society.

London has been kept warm, and dirty, for centuries by sea coal, coal brought by sea from mines in the north—loaded at Newcastle and other ports, and brought to London by that 'nursery of seamen', England's coasting trade. City churches consumed by the Fire of 1666 were rebuilt with money from an extra tax on sea coal, rising to become Byron's 'wilderness of steeples peeping/On tiptoe through their sea-coal canopy' of London smoke. Colliers today come down the east coast and steam upriver on the rising tide to unload at power stations serving London's gas and electricity boards and Underground trains, but there is no such fleet of colliers now as there was a century ago. In 1849, a maritime theme suited the splendid ceremonies arranged by the City of London for the last day of October, which must have been (unjustly) a clear day. A grand water pageant was held, the first of such splendour since William IV opened London Bridge in 1831, and the last official voyage for the carved and gilded Royal Barge (designed by William Kent in 1732, it is now in the Maritime Museum at Greenwich). In it Prince Albert and the two eldest Royal children (the Queen having chicken pox) embarked at Whitehall Stairs, near the sites of Whitehall Court and Horse Guards Avenue, and proceeded downriver to the Custom House quay accompanied by other elaborate barges of the Admiralty and the City companies (perhaps some of those that now keep different company on the Isis at Oxford). Steamers filled with spectators lined the route, masses of people packed into boats or elbowed on bridges and wharves, some even watched from the galleries of St Paul's, and the air was full of church bells, brass bands and cheers.

At the Coal Exchange itself, inside the new rotunda where a strange iron construction was almost obscured by the crowd of peers, aldermen, ambassadors and trumpeters, Prince Albert received with marked attention the City Architect who had designed it, James Bunstone Bunning. In the day's principal speech, by the Recorder of the City of London, the iron construction of the rotunda was not obscured: it was appropriate to build chiefly in iron, he said, when 'with the purposes of this Exchange are associated the creation and increase of commerce and manufactures, and the naval superiority of this kingdom [the era of iron ships was now begun] . . . when the

43

essential article of coal ministers by appliances innumerable to the wants and prosperity of millions . . . whenever metal at the forge is obedient to the fire it feeds, whilst it commands as its agent and its instrument the mighty power of steam.' And then they all sat down to luncheon—the Victorian ceremonial mode of opening a new building ever being to eat a meal in it. Wines were supplied by Domecq (that still flourishing source), the firm of Mr Ruskin senior. Ruskin, Telford & Domecq carried on their business nearby 'in a small counting-house on the first floor of narrow premises' (now rebuilt) near the Fenchurch Street end of Billiter Street, according to *Praeterita* and trade directories.

Young Mr Ruskin, whose *Seven Lamps of Architecture* had been published five months before, seems to have ignored the new Coal Exchange, for he detested the 'employment of metallic framework' as a 'departure from the first principles of the art' of true architecture, while reluctantly admitting that metallic construction might one day be suitable in some situations, structurally though not ornamentally. He added a homely simile, 'for it is in this license as in that of wine, a man may use it for his infirmities, but not for his nourishment'. A good thing for Bunning's ironwork, as for the Ruskin wine business, that the City of London disagreed.

But the City was ready to tolerate this rotunda's metallic framework only because it was well hidden from the street by wings of conventional masonry, held between them as in the jaws of a nutcracker, and approached through a neo-classic tower. Post-medieval street architecture usually consisted of load-bearing walls built up of one brick or stone laid upon another, sometimes with an outer skin of cement or costlier stone. The skeleton of Bunning's rotunda, fully visible indoors, was structurally independent of its infilling panels, so reverting in a sense to medieval timber-frame construction, whether he thought so or not. Bunning in fact, when making his design in 1846, is said to have taken a great interest in the iron-ribbed dome of the Halle au Blé or Granary in Paris, a pioneering work of the early nineteenth century, and perhaps an influence on other circular buildings of the mid-Forties in London: the London and North-Western Railway's Round House at Chalk Farm, with its open eye, designed by the engineer R. B. Dockray in 1846, and William Bradwell's refurbishing in 1845 of Burton's sixteen-sided Colosseum in Regent's Park with a ribbed dome holding embossed-glass panels. The Roman Pantheon was inevitably in their minds, part of the classic syllabus, as it were, as Virgil still was for poets.

So what did the Coal Factors' new cage look like? It is worth remembering, first for its conception, a gallant proposal for the handling of iron that went no further but might have changed Victorian handling of that material if it had, and second for its destruction, a landmark in twentieth-century vandalism.

The previous Coal Exchange of *c*. 1800, on another site, had had a skylighted central space. Skylights with small panes of glass were common enough then, and became more so by the Forties when larger glass sheets were available and many a bijou palace in the suburbs had its central toplit hall: after the great hailstorm of August 1846, the universal greeting was not 'How's your family?' but 'How's your skylights?' (*ILN*, 8 August 1846). In the new iron-ribbed Pantheon, its dome ribs held thick panels of roughened plate glass, rising to a large central eye of amber glass, the line of these ribs being carried down by stanchions to the floor. There were three tiers of galleries with glass panelling giving added light to surrounding offices, and narrow wall panels painted with suitable coal-mining scenes and symbols.

The principal, decorative feature, the casting of the iron stanchions with loops and coils of rope ornament (*Fig. 10*), struck a marine note when coal still arrived under sail. 'Architecture in cordage,' sniffed one foreign visitor. That twisting cast iron cable-work was in the City tradition of exuberant ornament, yet much more original and allusive than the fruity garlands on livery company halls of Wren's day. It was in the salty tradition of seaside exuberance, too. This rope ornament, like that so liberally applied to buildings of maritime Portugal in the era of Magellan and Vasco da Gama, celebrated sea power. And technically, such cable moulding was traditionally suited to iron casting; one sees it on Tudor firebacks. The structural and ornamental use of iron here must have involved close collaboration from the start between architect and builder and the firm of ironsmiths in Old Street that supplied the iron members. The ironworking firm could not have been brought in after the design was made.

If this was 'decorated construction' (Owen Jones's much-parroted formula of the Fifties, in his *Grammar of Ornament*: 'Construction should be Decorated, and Decoration should never be purposely Constructed'), it was decoration that took the material into account. (Consider the iron classical columns (*Fig. 11*) that were much more common.) The nature of materials was not likely to be pursued in a society where the Ironmongers' Company refitted its

45

Fig. 10 *Coal Exchange: inspired ironwork*

banquet room with 'truly magnificent' papier maché panelling imitating oak in the Elizabethan style (*ILN*, 1 May 1847). Papier maché was thought to be interesting as 'an extraordinary application of the steam-engine to decorative art' (*ILN*, 16 October 1847). Technique was all. The mighty power of steam, the gigantic power of steam, was as new as electronics to us.

A new arena—the exhibition building—was soon to exploit a gardener's attitude toward glass and iron, in which glass was the vital principle. In the Coal Exchange rotunda, iron was the active material structurally and ornamentally, glass was only part of the infill. This domed and doomed space, entirely an interior, outwardly visible only from the top of the Monument or a nearby church tower, was a theatre in the round with the audience confined to the galleries or, to look at it another way, in full participation in the daily ritual of the exchange: the crowd of top-hatted men arguing the price of coal with one eye on the wind-indicator, the state of the

Fig. 11 *Gresham Street: conventional ironwork*

wind (until steam supplanted sail) swaying affairs by showing how
soon certain shiploads would be in and so how long negotiations
could be spun out. No other City exchange housed itself so allu-
sively, so originally. This interesting cage was worth more than the
few feet of highway for which it was demolished in 1962.

In 1848–9, while revolutions rolled on the Continent and Mivart's
(later merged in Claridge's) Hotel in Brook Street filled with the
de-crowned heads of Europe—they still make for it—London had
two autumns of cholera. At last it was being slowly realized that
this was a disease of filth. 'The dirtiest old spots in the dirtiest old
towns under the worst old governments in Europe' were not worse
than London, Dickens told a public meeting afterwards. 'Vested
rights in crowded houses, deadly stenches, putrid water, foggy
courts, and cesspools' (*Household Words*, 1850) might not be sacred
to private landlords after all. That vested private rights in murderous
surroundings were sacred in some quarters still in the Sixties, we

47

shall see in that chapter. Meanwhile, the 'perpetual surging and heaving of local jealousies and animosities' in a metropolis whose growth was 'one of the most extraordinary things in an extraordinary age' (*ILN*, 15 December 1849) made reform difficult, and private associations had to be the first to try out the model lodgings, the model houses for families. Private cussedness could only be countered by private initiative.

The great parishes of London outside the City walls up until 1855 had no effective local government powers over bad landlords at all (and we shall see in the Sixties how little they had then). Even in the City, rebuilding of houses as warehouses and offices meant greater overcrowding for the poor who still multiplied there: vivid reports of their lives and deaths by the City's Medical Officer of Health, Dr John Simon, made grim reading for those who noticed. 'Never had there been a time . . . in which land-owners, house-owners, and builders did as freely as they liked with their own, regardless of the injury or damage inflicted upon others . . . no period when the spirit of commercialism recked so little of the physical condition and circumstances of those on whom, after all, it depended' (Jephson, *The Sanitary Evolution of the Metropolis*, 1907).

Yet in 1848 one far-sighted practical step was taken in extending the Ordnance Survey—the mapping of the country by an expert Army department—to London; for without determining the precise levels of London's topography no sense could ever be made of the chaos of its drainage. In the spring of 1848, crow's-nests for the surveyors 'levelling the Metropolis', as *Punch* put it, were rigged up on one of Westminster Abbey's towers, St Paul's dome, and other points of vantage; *Punch* reported one old lady supposing these scaffolds were for firing cannon upon Chartists, whose attempt to march on London failed in April. But *Punch* was pollution-conscious in 1848: 'thousands of us are going up and down by penny boats . . . persons of repute go and dine at Greenwich. . . . Whither are we to fly? . . . Death lurks in my pot at home . . . the air is poisoned; life is poisoned; business is poisoned; pleasure is poisoned.'

South London, with its larger area of low-lying flood-plain within the great Thames meander from Greenwich to Battersea, suffered most from cholera. In 1849 both the Lambeth and the Southwark Water Companies were still pumping water from the Thames, the former near the south end of Hungerford Bridge, almost opposite the Northumberland Street sewer outlet. In the parishes around Elephant and Castle in the autumn of 1849, bells tolled continually while empty coffins were delivered like parcels on the heads of running men who knocked on doors like postmen (*ILN*, 27 October 1849). It was appallingly obvious that London could not keep its own house in order. 'Our great sins as a community are ignorance, indifference, and cupidity . . . an artificial barbarism has grown up', declared the *Illustrated London News*, not needing later generations' hindsight; uncleanliness led to pestilence because water and air and light were luxuries to the poor, the plague was a penalty for selfishness (*ILN*, 17 November 1849). Bland descriptions of London's water supply offered in popular handbooks on the Metropolis prepared for the year of the Great Exhibition, doubtless based on copy provided by the private water companies concerned, are quite wonderful when compared with Dr Simon's forthright accusation of 'criminal indifference to the public safety' by, especially, the Southwark & Vauxhall Company as late as 1866, when more cholera arrived.

And yet, at home and abroad, the British felt themselves to be, far more than any other people, 'the messengers of civilization': all over the world 'we have left our beneficent marks. . . . Our physical, moral, and intellectual presence is felt in every region of the globe' (*ILN*, 13 October 1849). A sense of the past and of the future, of existing uniquely between them, was stirred whenever ancient remains turned up in the hurly-burly of rebuilding the City, a compost heap if ever there was one (for example, the Roman bath found on the site of the Coal Exchange, all we have left there now): 'London has its Pompeii and Herculaneum. Unnumbered generations have trampled into dust their splendour . . . lying as far beneath our feet as we in intellectual arts have towered above their former possessors. We belong to the future, as they do to the present; and when we perish, our glory will be found lettered in every corner of the rounded globe' (*ILN*, 28 April 1849). New offices then being completed for that insurance company so appropriately named Imperial Assurance, at the corner of Broad and Threadneedle Streets (now demolished), bore prominent keystones over the ground floor windows carved by John Thomas as bearded heads symbolizing Power, Fire, Water, The City, and so on. This feature so much followed on London buildings may not in this case necessarily, or entirely, stem from the architect John Gibson's study of Renaissance examples in Verona or on the Strand front of Somerset House, but from the supposition that ancient Romans had used it. Victorian imperial assurance was bolstered by such models.

E

Commercial crisis has been weathered at home, 'a total change in the water-economy of London' would slowly come, a Great Exhibition of the Works of Industry of All Nations had been proposed by Prince Albert and a site for it already chosen in Hyde Park (as announced in Henry Cole's *Journal of Design*). Britain desired only 'peace with the whole world, and trade with whomsoever we can procure it' (*ILN*, 3 November 1849). That was evident as far away as Constantinople:

> English crockery is everywhere . . . and the old blue willow pattern constantly meets the eye. You can also buy . . . Burgess's mixed pickles .·. . Rowland's macassar oil, and pale ale and stout. . . . And as I started in a steamer . . . from the Golden Horn, to go up to Buyukdere, near the Black Sea, amidst the din of tongues, I looked down a hatchway and saw the inscription, 'J. Penn & Son, Engineers, Greenwich', in honest English, upon the engines. They cannot do without us. (*ILN*, 20 October 1849)

Yet the unsettled state of the Continent kept most tourists at home: 'It's a comfort to think that one's purse/Is the one thing that bleeds, down at Brighton', sang *Punch* in 1848. London tradesmen oozed confidence, in their advertisements anyway, like this tailor-and-draper of the Minories:

> While nearly all the civil world
> In dread confusion has been hurl'd
> . . . happily we still retain
> Victoria's unmolested reign.
> Commerce and trade once more revive
> And promise speedily to thrive.
> Moses and Son, amid the stir,
> Are firmer than they ever were.
> And like Victoria, they can say,
> They grow in confidence each day.
>
> (*ILN*, 30 December 1848)

More money for investing in property, and feeing lawyers, slowly accrued.

So here was the Metropolis at mid-century, seething and festering and spreading: enormous smoking London, driving, hurrying, marrying, burying; fog up the river, fog down the river, everywhere a stirring multitude and a great crush and crash of carts and wains, everywhere a perpetual surging and heaving of local jealousies and animosities; and at the heart of it all, lawyers in their offices like maggots in nuts—to echo Thackeray, Tennyson, Dickens, Disraeli, the *Illustrated London News*, and again Dickens as summoned up in this chapter. Behind the company promoters, eager investors, earnest architects, and local vestries anxious or apathetic, were lawyers among their boxes labelled with many names, guiding capital in search of property and property in search of capital, even more than bankers entrusted and encrusted with secrets, spinning webs in quiet corners, the real ground landlords of London.

CHAPTER THREE

The Fifties:
Arrivers and Developers

The flavour of all the arrivals and developments stirring in London suburbs in the Fifties is best conveyed by sampling one suburb. So let us take Clapham, a mile and a half south of the Thames and four miles south-west of the City, in what was then Surrey. In 1851, the five domestic servants at the Cedars, an Early Georgian house in its own large grounds on the north side of Clapham Common, reported on the Census paper that they came, respectively, from Uttoxeter, Dover, Alnwick, Dumfries, and Hastings. Between 1851 and 1855, the house was occupied, possibly as a country retreat, by George Head (electoral registers), possibly Sir George Head, deputy knight marshal to the Queen and writer of travel books, born in Kent, died in 1855. The Cedars land, about seventeen acres, was bought in 1853 as an investment, with a view to ripening value when Chelsea Bridge opened due north of it, by a successful Southwark tradesman named Jones. In Clapham's earlier and more spacious days, one of its eminences, William Wilberforce, had observed that cutting up land for houses was rather like cutting up a haunch of venison into mutton chops. Nevertheless, it was Jones's turn.

The career of Alexander Jones neatly illustrates the social history latent in post office directories and census reports. Born in Whitechapel about 1803, he turned up in the Old Kent Road in Southwark where he and his wife (from Norfolk) had children in the Twenties. Migration from Whitechapel was only a matter of walking past Aldgate Pump and down Fenchurch Street to cross London Bridge, and then down the Borough High Street to the Dover Road, or Old Kent Road, a principal thoroughfare to and from London's oldest bridge. There he was a tailor until 1846, living over the shop beside the Bricklayers' Arms, the public house from which the nearby railway terminus was named in 1844. From 1847 Jones was out of the directories entirely for three years (Australia? having, perhaps, during the railway mania year, 1846, made money out of other men's speculation?). At any rate, he seems to have been the same person who turned up in 1850 as a bill broker living in Union Crescent, New Kent Road, just round the corner from his old shop, and then in 1851, after moving across New Kent Road to the grander Paragon, dropping out of the trade directory for good and into the Court Guide for 1852 as an esquire. He then bought the Cedars property, abetted by his son-in-law, a City merchant (1849) turned commission-agent (1853). Jones never lived on his Clapham property himself. Two of his servants in 1851, incidentally, had been born in the Old Kent Road; it was not entirely an immigrant neighbourhood.

When, at the end of the Fifties, the Cedars land was considered ripe for development as a new road of new houses, two more people were drawn in. One was the ground landlord's architect, who furnished a set of designs and over the next decade certified the speculating builder's right to his leases. The architect was James T. Knowles Jr, future editor of the *Nineteenth Century* review, aged 28 and living with his parents in a stuccoed mansion in Clapham Park designed by his father; he and his father had been born in Reigate, his mother at Rotherhithe (and their servants at Rugby, Exeter, Marlborough, and Charlbury). The risk-taking builder was Henry Harris (whose origins are less easy to discover); he had been building on Cubitt's developments in Pimlico and Clapham Park. In the Sixties, when property uphill but downwind from the open Heath-wall sewer 'moved' slowly, until that poisonous ditch was covered in, some of Harris's Cedars Road leases were taken by his solicitor, George Jeremiah Mayhew of Great George Street, Westminster (possibly a connection of Henry Mayhew, though not apparently of the latter's family firm).

If we look into the decade after the conception of this development, the complicated texture of property conveyance is suggested by other names involved with just one of the Cedars Road villas and its garden. Initially it was mortgaged to F. H. Brandram, then of St Leonard's but possibly of the family that developed part of Lewisham. The first occupier was the widow of John Allnutt, the wine merchant who had bought pictures from Constable and Turner for his private collection at Clapham Common; the second occupier was George P. Bidder Jr, barrister, son of the celebrated civil

53

engineer (and grandfather of the historian Dr Kitson Clark). Property on the road behind, bought to extend the back garden, had been mortgaged to Atkinson Morley, sometime proprietor of Morley's Hotel in Trafalgar Square and the Burlington Hotel in Cork Street, who died in 1858 leaving £100,000 to found the hospital at Wimbledon that bears his name.

The myriad artisans and tradesmen concerned with these houses in the Sixties probably included James McLachlan, initially a 'decorator, gilder, and ornamental painter' of St James's, Westminster, and Clapham; he was building for Knowles elsewhere at the time, and probably did some elaborate ornamental painting in one of the big terrace houses on the Common. McLachlan was to become a substantial Clapham vestryman and builder, by 1870 taking seventy of his men on the annual August outing to the Lion at Farningham, Kent, in three four-horse buses, and later in the Seventies building for Norman Shaw on Chelsea Embankment.

This recital of a few of the names—and only a few, omitting district and parish surveyors and most of the lawyers—involved in one small piece of South London development, affords some sense of the sheer human density of the network of suburban property transactions in Victorian London. The physical remains of this particular network today are Cedars Road SW4 with most of its villas gone, and no remains of St Saviour's church bombed in the last war, but with the twin terraces still facing the Common—less beetling of cornice than once they were, first cousins to the Grosvenor Hotel at Victoria, concocted by the Knowleses at the end of the Fifties (next chapter). Both the ground landlord's design for investment and the architect's designs for houses were very much the fruit of the Fifties, gathered with the gusto appropriate to the brink of the Sixties. And 'it is to be doubted whether there is a successful tradesman amongst us who does not look forward to purchasing a freehold. . . . [With] this English fondness for the acquisition of the soil of our country . . . there is always going amongst us [this] process of transmutation of real property' (according to the *Illustrated London News*, 22 February 1862). Outside the limits of the great estates that held so much of central London, the clop-clop of the successful tradesman's horses (echoing those of Tennyson's Northern Farmer) said property-property-property in London accents.

If it is unheard-of to begin a chapter on London in the 1850s without first mentioning the Great Exhibition of 1851 (*Fig. 12*),

Fig. 12 *Crystal Palace, Hyde Park, interior in 1851*

these were some of the people who went to it, a-stare with surprise
—Londoners wherever they had been born, pleased to find London
'the theatre of an event of the highest moral importance', as one
up-to-the-minute guidebook put it. Guidebooks to the Metropolis
multiplied in the summer of the Great Exhibition, not only for
foreign and provincial sightseers (the *Oxford English Dictionary*
finds 'sight-seer' first in 1847, though 'tourist' goes back to 1800),
but also for new Londoners who might ordinarily see few sights
outside their adopted parishes. The insularity of Londoners was
often remarked, not one anthill but many, 'not a city but a nation'.
The population of the Metropolis in 1851 was about two and a
half million (depending again which measure of its area one used).

The Crystal Palace 'rose like an exhalation' (Victorians quoting
Milton) or an assembly of prefabricated parts (modern hindsight)
in a few months. Glazing was begun in December 1850, but soon
after Paxton's design was adopted in July, *Punch* began feeling for
a name: this 'Glass Palace' would have 'the lightness of crystal'
(August 24); 'Mr Paxton's glass palace' would shelter even Irish
exhibits 'beneath the hospitable roof of crystal' (October 12);
foreigners were to have the conceit taken out of them by 'the Crystal
Palace' (November 2). 'Empirical Palace' it might have been called,
with its transept arching over the elms as a saving afterthought of
Paxton's design. The site, now grassy playing fields, lay along the
road to Kensington just west of the old Knightsbridge Barracks (of
1795) and south of that whale-shaped body of water the Serpentine,
only temporarily cleansed of sewage. The south front was but a
few yards from the Kensington road; most published views—on
everything from souvenir saucers to souvenir handkerchiefs—
showed the north front with Park and Serpentine spread out before
it. The south entrance was nearly opposite Prince's Gate (now
Prince of Wales Gate) with its stuccoed lodges and lamp-crowned
piers. A dozen or so new occupiers of bran-new stuccoed terraces on
the south side of Kensington Road, opposite the Exhibition, must
have had their fill of crowds by the time the whole business was
over. The pair of park lodges still mark the approximate midpoint
in the Palace's great length of 1848 feet—about as long as Portland
Place or roughly four times the internal length of St Paul's.

Exhibits of the Industry of All Nations were assembled in the
early months of 1851. Between the fanfare day of its opening on
May 1 and the closing ceremony on October 15, the Great Exhibition was seen by about six million visitors. A few of the more critical

noted 'a total want of profiles' on the exterior of the great glass shed, but inside, 'the endless perspective, the sea of light above and of people below, the thousands upon thousands of beautiful and precious objects' combined 'in one magnificence, which subdues the mind in a moment' (a Dutch visitor reported by the *Builder*, 18 October 1851). The Exhibition was closed as it had been opened by a sacramental rendering of Handel's Hallelujah Chorus, prelude to years of Handel's music ringing among the glassy vaults at Sydenham.

There on a rural hill with a wide view of Kent countryside—not yet swaddled in suburbs—the temporary pavilion from Hyde Park was reincarnated in more permanent form during the years 1852–4 (*Fig. 13*). Shortened in length but much heightened, with three arched transepts (the northern one destroyed by fire in 1866), it was solidly rooted with a brick basement for heating-pipes taking up the incline from the brow of the hill, and it was flanked by two water towers (almost immediately rebuilt when the first pair proved unsafe), eventually providing the head of power for great fountains in the elaborately landscaped gardens. 'A cucumber frame between two chimneys', said Ruskin, watching from his old suburb how the new palace dwarfed the Norwood hills into 'three long lumps of clay,

Fig. 13 *Crystal Palace, Sydenham, under construction*

on lease for building'. Even before the formal opening of the Sydenham Crystal Palace by the Queen in June 1854, journalists noted the rise in land values around it, with the branch railway from the Brighton Line to London Bridge soon to open: 'A new world of houses seems to start from the ground all around it,' remarked the *Art Journal* in April. The coincidence has been remarked that the original owner of much of the Crystal Palace site at Sydenham was a director of the London, Brighton & South Coast Railway Company.

The contents of the new winter garden included among the potted plants a great deal of sculpture in the form of plaster casts of works ancient and modern, and a series of Architectural Courts intended to provide three-dimensional art education—a series of separate side-shows, as it were, within the great nave. These extended the idea of Pugin's Medieval Court, brought from Hyde Park, and included the Alhambra Court of Lions done to half-scale from the original in Spain; the designer Owen Jones a decade before had brought out three elephant folios of Alhambra details that were a landmark of colour-printing. An Architectural Museum founded in 1852 in Westminster, in an old 'cock-loft' in Cannon Row by the site of New Scotland Yard, to inspire 'art-feeling' among architects and artisans by models of architectural details, was also a source of inspiration for the Courts at Sydenham. One can still form an enjoyably melancholy notion of what it was like to be surrounded by so many casts of the world's sculpture in two large courts at the Victoria and Albert Museum where a surrealist flock of such things have come to rest.

A quite different set of re-creations still lurk at the bottom of the garden at Sydenham: the prehistoric monsters in stone on the shores of the lake near the Penge gate. On 31 December 1853, only a dozen years after the word 'dinosaur' was invented, and only a few more since Gideon Mantell had found and named fossil remains of the giant lizard, Iguanodon, in the Sussex Weald, twenty-two eminent scientists sat down to dinner in the lower half of a full-size model of the Iguanodon in the studio of the model-maker, Mr Waterhouse Hawkins, at the still unopened Crystal Palace. The tone at Sydenham was to be like that, educational yet convivial.

When the Palace was working at full stretch, there was nothing to equal it. For example, a gathering of the National Temperance League in the 1860s would draw 30,000 people on railway excursions run from York, Lancashire, Cornwall, and the South Coast (by then the Crystal Palace had two railway stations), to a programme including 'Great Fountains, Choral Concert of 3000 Voices, Public Meetings, Balloon Ascent', everything. Over the years, much was made of the concerts and out of the programme notes by George Grove, Secretary to the Crystal Palace Company (and much else) grew the indispensable Grove's *Dictionary of Music and Musicians*. Piercing notes cracked no glass, apparently. Not only acres of glass roofs but the glass fountain, provided by Osler's of Birmingham and Oxford Street for the Hyde Park interior, vibrated for some eighty years to all those oratorios rendered by massed choirs looking like the Day of Judgment. Judgment Day arrived in the great fire of 1936, seen all over south-eastern England and even by air-pilots over the Channel. Next day the iron framework still standing amidst the wreckage must have resembled Paxton's first rough drawing on a piece of blotting-paper in June 1850. Ironically enough, the most splendid of its outdoor displays from 1865 on were fireworks, great set-pieces of naval battles, the Battle of Trafalgar 820 feet across, and in the Palace's last years, the Battle of Jutland. Opened in the first brave months of the Crimean War, the Sydenham Crystal Palace expired just before Edward VIII's abdication. It had given a great many people a wonderful time.

The transient predecessor in Hyde Park left its own legacy. The surplus profits of the 1851 Exhibition were invested in the purchase of land south of Kensington Gore, on which were eventually built the Albert Hall, the South Kensington (later Victoria and Albert) Museum, and the Natural History Museum (all Chapter 4), the Imperial Institute (Chapter 6), and in this century the Science Museum and the Geology Museum, to mention only the larger institutions there—like Whitehall, and the neighbourhood of the Royal Exchange, one of the most influential concentrations of activity in the world.

That was to be slow accretion. The fabric of London in 1851, save for a few new single buildings, and new residential quarters filling in empty spaces and swelling the outskirts, was still largely Georgian. A popular panoramic engraving of 1849 showing the way from Parliament Square to the top of Regent Street reeled off a ribbon of almost entirely Georgian buildings, with only three exceptions. John Tallis's new views of main streets in 1847 had shown little change in the character of, for example, Fleet Street save for an insurance company at No. 50 (*Fig. 3*) on the site of the present Norwich Union building of 1911. The rebuilding of the

59

old domesticated counting-houses and warehouses in the City gathered momentum during the Fifties as the merchants living upstairs moved to Sydenham, say, or Gospel Oak. The Royal Academy summer exhibition in 1853 suddenly included eight designs for office buildings after only one the year before (not all for London, nor were all such designs shown there). But there was a stabilizer enforcing a Georgian equilibrium upon the neighbourhoods west of the City: the long-term leasehold grip exerted by the great estates, Bedford, Grosvenor, Portman, and so on. So Podsnaps lived in shady angles adjoining a completely Georgian Portman Square and Boffinses moved up in the world to the neighbourhood of an un-Victorianized Cavendish Square, whatever scorn Victorian architects felt for Georgian hole-in-the-wall windows and the bald sameness of Georgian streets. Thackeray might call Wimpole Street 'a dingy Mausoleum of the genteel' in the Forties, but Gladstone found Georgian Harley Street convenient when out of office in the Seventies. The Veneerings, of course, lived in a bran-new house in a bran-new quarter of London, not necessarily of the moment *Our Mutual Friend* was written, perhaps even Brompton, where there had been 'a great brick-and-mortar stir' with houses 'rising up like whole streets in a pantomime' in the Forties, or perhaps 'the new Squares and Terraces of the brilliant bran-new Bayswater-and-Tyburnia' (*Punch*, Thackeray). New quarters like this—in a word, Stuccovia—were described by one seasoned Londoner, John Hollingshead, in terms we have heard used of some modern housing estates (for stucco, read concrete):

> I detest a modern, well-advertised building estate . . . a man must be perpetually struggling . . . to preserve his individuality in such a settlement . . . it may be warmed up by thorough occupation; perambulators may be seen in its bare new squares; broughams may stand by the side of its bright level kerbstones; but the demon of sameness, in my eyes, would always be brooding over it. . . .
> I should die of a surfeit of stucco. . . . There can be little pleasure in contemplating cold stucco porticoes of a mongrel Greek type . . . or lines of oven-like foundations waiting for more capital and more enterprise to cover them with houses. (*Cornhill Magazine*, April 1860)

Much house-building around Hyde Park was stimulated by the Exhibition of 1851. The new development opposite the Crystal Palace, the series of terraces called Prince's Gate, were large stuccoed five-storey Anglo-Italian houses on their own approach road parallel to Kensington Road, and eventually extending down Exhibition Road. This investment may have been the result of some smart footwork by the developer as soon as the Exhibition site was chosen in 1849. At any rate, using only post office directories, there were three occupiers in 1850 (including a major-general), twelve in 1851, twenty-one in 1853, and by the end of the decade thirty houses were occupied. The present No. 14, with its American Indian-head keystones over the ground floor windows, belonged to the Morgan banking family as early as the 1850s and was later the American Embassy (plaque to John F. Kennedy).

The builder of some or all of these houses is said to have been John Elger, who had been operating in Kensington Road for some time (*ILN*, 29 August 1846) and did so well out of the spurt of building in the Fifties that by 1857 he was listed only in the Court Guide section of the directory, as Elger esquire residing in Rutland Gate. He was one of the undertakers of the Victoria Station Bill of 1857–8 and subsequently a director of the Victoria Station and Pimlico Railway Company (next chapter). Elger's tame architect is said to have been the John Johnson, or one of them, who keeps turning up in minor Mid-Victorian building history. The developer is said to have been (later Sir) Charles James Freake, who developed Onslow Square, part of Cromwell Road, and much else. In short, Prince's Gate was a usual sort of development, save for its initially prominent position right in front of the Crystal Palace. It was also somewhat unusual in that civilized feature the private approach road, or corporate town version of the suburban carriage drive, only possible with a good depth of frontage; that was also a feature of Sussex Gardens and Westbourne Terrace of the Forties.

The greater height of ceilings in new houses had partly to do with the heat generated by increasingly elaborate gasoliers (*Fig. 14*). But larger causes of larger houses were more people with expanding incomes, more rising jostling fortunes wishing to be seen as solidly based, and a steady stream of young servant material coming up to London from the country. The difference between 1840 and 1860 in the scale of town houses can be seen by standing in front of the Victoria and Albert Museum and comparing Thurloe Square oppo-site with the south side of Cromwell Road off to the right (or in the illustrations to Dorothy Stroud's little history of the Thurloe Estate, 1965).

The stuccoed mountain ranges (as they seemed then) north and south of the Park and elsewhere were simply the old London

Fig. 14 *Cedars Terrace, Clapham : suburban drawing room*

terrace, row, or block of uniform houses (with or without accented ends and centre), writ large. Terraces like widening ripples from a cast stone had been palisading London ever since the seventeenth century, with the few set variations in plan, conditioned by depth and width of site, that all Londoners know. The level of back garden or yard is generally about halfway between the built-up street level and the excavated basement level with its front and back outdoor 'areas' affording light and air for the basement. Along the ordinary central London street without front gardens, there runs the railed-off and compartmented dry moat of front areas, each originally with its gate and flight of steps for tradesmen to the kitchen door under the bridge of the front doorstep. In the front wall of each area a door led to the coal cellar under the public pavement, hence those cast iron coal hole covers for noisy delivery directly through the pavement. 'The area' is part of folklore: *Punch* jokes about the butcher's boy or Cook's friend the police constable, T. S. Eliot on damp souls of housemaids. Chimney-sweeps (part of London folklore too) having to arrive before the fires were lit might come before the maids sleeping in the attic were up; hence the label 'sweeps' bell' until recently to be seen on a doorpost in York Street, Marylebone, and probably connecting originally with the attic (see John Leech, 'Domestic bliss' series, on maids unable to hear the sweep ringing at dawn, *Punch*, 4 September 1847). The front area is now the sunken garden of many an expensive basement flat, with the scullery maid's view of the moon through area railings blocked off by parked cars on the pavement.

Terrace housing was not all. The long block vertically sliced, with housemaid's walking distance kitchen-to-attic as much as ten flights of stairs (two flights and a landing per storey), had a foreign alternative familiar in Scotland which first in all its horizontal independence appeared in London in the Fifties, in Victoria Street. The word 'flat' was still being placed in quotation marks by some estate agents in the Seventies, but already appeared without them in professional literature in 1852 when the first block was begun (and the *Oxford English Dictionary* finds the word, in the sense of a complete suite on one floor, as early as 1824 though not for London). A loquacious octogenarian architect, George Ledwell Taylor, writing his memoirs in 1870, claimed that in 1830, when he built the east side of Trafalgar Square (soon to become, in part, Morley's Hotel): 'I had laid out the buildings in *flats*.' He was talking of what were probably chambers, apartments to let or, as we might say, service flats. Indeed one basis for Henry Ashton's plans of 1852 'on the Scotch principle' for Victoria Street was surely the simple type of the sets of legal chambers in, say, Raymond Buildings, Gray's Inn, of 1825. Ashton placed his flats on either side of a spinal 'stair tower' (not articulated as such outside) much like that earlier arrangement. *Blackwood's Magazine* published an article recommending French horizontal living (June 1846, perhaps only to be expected of a periodical published in Edinburgh), and pointed out that the French system encouraged architectural display and solid construction, whereas the English vertical system encouraged cheap, shabby-genteel, slightly built houses. Be that as it may. Ashton's five-storey blocks on the south side of Victoria Street (demolished 1971) were protected by a model lodging house for the working class behind them, from a view of the New Bridewell (House of Correction) on the site of Westminster Cathedral (Chapter 7). In Ashton's blocks the pattern for Victoria Street was set (possibly by the Westminster Improvement Commissioners administering the new street and letting sites to speculators): the eighty-foot cornice height and the ground floor and entresol pattern for shops, the latter a Continental fashion that went back to the ancient Romans and more nearly to Louis Napoléon's Paris, although these stuccoed invisible-roofed blocks were entirely in character with English work of the early Fifties. At first they attracted some tenants 'from the highest

63

class of society', yet further development did not proceed until the Sixties: Victoria Street was not yet ripe.

In spite of all this building of whole flanks of streets, commentators in 1851 noted a trend to detached-house building. At the grand end of the scale, noblemen's town palaces had always been rare in England: most peers preferred to spend money on their country houses and were content with terrace houses in town, with a few grandiose exceptions such as the Duke of Sutherland's Stafford House (now Lancaster House; after a chequered history, finished by Barry in the early Forties) and the Earl of Ellesmere's Bridgwater House by Barry (1841, 1846–54), and in the late Fifties William Burn designed a new Montagu House in Whitehall for the Duke of Buccleuch.

One palatial free-standing house was being built for a commoner: Dorchester House in Park Lane for Robert Stainer Holford, a connoisseur in possession of an inherited fortune, and advised, it is said, by his brother-in-law, Sir Coutts Lindsay, who later founded the Grosvenor Gallery. Holford's architect was Lewis Vulliamy (1791–1871), son of a celebrated Georgian clockmaker, a pupil of Robert Smirke, and a seasoned practioner in several architectural styles since the Twenties. Contractors for the building of Dorchester House were the firm of William Cubitt, brother of Thomas Cubitt. William retired from business in 1854, served as an M.P. in 1847–61 and 1862–3, was twice Lord Mayor and tremendously rich (he was not William Cubitt the civil engineer, one of the Commissioners for the 1851 Exhibition).

Dorchester House dominated the south half of Park Lane until it was replaced in 1930 by the Dorchester Hotel. Outwardly based partly on the Villa Farnesina in Rome, with the long side toward Park Lane, this great villa's Portland stone elegance excited much interest by 1852 when the exterior was almost finished; it was, rather, a town palace like Stafford House and others less dazzling on Park Lane (see Augustus Hare's sketch at head of this chapter). By 1856, the interior with its great arcaded staircase-hall (*Fig. 15*), like a terrace-stepped inner courtyard, was complete enough for Holford to move in. A few years later began the famous interior decoration by the painter, sculptor, and metalwork designer Alfred Stevens (1817–75) in a rich Renaissance manner re-created by himself; fragments of this work, chimneypieces, mirrors, sculpture, survive at the Tate Gallery, at the Walker Art Gallery in Liverpool, and in many drawings at the Victoria and Albert Museum. Stevens's

Fig. 15 *Dorchester House: the staircase in 1910*

most important existing work is the Wellington Monument in St Paul's Cathedral. Replicas of his little cast iron lion appear, sitting up straight, on railings in various parts of London (in front of the Law Society in Chancery Lane, on the Georgian railings of Ely House in Dover Street), and in rather debased form in other materials in many a suburban garden.

Great mansions were rare, flats were new-fangled, continuous terraces went on being built for a maximum return on rents from limited ground space. But all around London in the suburbs was the villa, its pre-Victorian course from *villegiatura* to various degrees of semi-detachment already run. While London's villas first paired off in a planned multiplied way in St John's Wood in the 1790s, the cottage-pair in the country or on the high streets of London's outer villages had been sharing a party wall for some time. Victorian villa semi-detachment reached its nadir when two 'villa' fronts shared one gable, their party wall, as it were, carrying the common ridge-piece between two lean-to roofs. Byron Villa/Shakspere Villa on Battersea Park Road is still an example of that, with a rather gallantly pathetic picturesqueness of stucco machicolation along the gable. (In the Sixties, the occupier of the Shakspere Villa half was Samuel

65

Fig. 16 *Brandram Road, Lee: suburban close-set villas*

Poupart, a market gardener on what was to be the site of the Shaftesbury Park development in the Seventies—like all market gardeners
around London then, watching the march of roads and railways
across the fields of his livelihood. A Poupart firm still markets
vegetables at Covent Garden, no longer grown at Battersea.) Sometimes a suburban development was bravely begun with a 'model
double villa' and then the developer took a hard look at the waste
space on the sides, enforced by the villas' returning eaves, and
decided that a higher return on rents was to be got from continuous
terraces. Sometimes terraces were given a quasi-detached look
(*Figs. 16, 17*).

For the expanding middle class of the Fifties, the *rus in urbe* idea
merged with the separate (or almost separate) mansion idea as the
desirable prescription for a new house. Close-packed rows of dignified separate villas in the vicinity of Pembridge Square, Notting
Hill Gate, show how little margin detachment might have, barely
enough for gardeners to walk single-file between the houses (in
Pembridge Gardens, for example, built in 1858). Such close rows of
villas like chopped terraces still for the most part observed the civility
of blind side-walls in the interests of privacy (and, before 1851, of
the window tax), a civility later abandoned in many English and
American suburbs in the interests of light and air and easier planning, but partially preserved on some well-managed estates. Records
of one house of 1854 in Kensington Palace Gardens, with a neighbour only on its north side and a minimum of north windows, show

66

Fig. 17 *The Terrace, Champion Hill: suburban semi-terrace*

much pacifying of the neighbour going on both in 1854 and during alterations in 1937. The ancient lights principle cannot be invoked for almost simultaneous structures.

The place, indeed, where the scaled-down freestanding palace and the scaled-up single and paired villa first met and mingled in London was Kensington Palace Gardens, half a mile or so west of the 1851 Exhibition site. As early as 1841 the Office of Woods and Works had been making plans to lease the former kitchen garden of Kensington Palace for high-class residential development: an area (very roughly) 200 yards wide by 500 yards long, or just over twenty acres. They were far-sighted enough to realize that 'the palace in a garden', where the Queen had been born and brought up, no longer stood beside a village in the country. A new north–south road, called at first Queen's Road, was laid out from the Uxbridge (Bayswater) Road across this land and the Palace Green south of it, to Kensington Road (now High Street). Only the kitchen garden land north-west of the Palace, screened from the royal relatives' windows by the royal stables, was laid out for development. Twenty plots, not the total available, were taken as a speculation by J. M. Blashfield, the mosaic and terracotta manufacturer, whose prosperity was only temporarily checked by the bankruptcy of 1847 that terminated his interest here. In general, this development was hampered by the financial stresses of the Forties. But by 1851, when the Great Exhibition opened, about thirteen houses were occupied, including five facing the Uxbridge Road, and others apparently stood empty in carcass. By mid-1854, all but two of the ultimate twenty-nine houses in this enclave seem to have been built and occupied, or about to be occupied. London was slowly marching westward. Occupiers in 1854 included Samuel Morton Peto at No. 12, and at No. 19 Thomas Grissell his cousin and former partner, the builder of both houses to designs from the Barry offices; and there was the M.P. Charles Lushington at No. 1, the publisher Bevis Ellerby Green of Longmans etc. & Green at No. 5, Russell Gurney the Recorder of the City of London at No. 8, with a Spanish merchant at 8A, and Lord Harrington at No. 13.

The earliest estate layouts for Kensington Palace Gardens stipulated in generalized block form two facing rows of large semi-detached pairs, probably because the estate architect, James Pennethorne, had worked under Nash, adapting the old paired-villas idea of St John's Wood for Regent's Park and the Park Villages, although Pennethorne was purely an administrator, not a designer, for the Kensington development. A few of the first houses conformed to this idea, some outwardly symmetrical, some not. Though so near the old brick Palace, the new houses were to be 'faced with Cement colored and jointed to imitate Stone, or with white or yellow Brick of the best quality and Stone dressings'; that is, this provision was set in the early Forties. In the end, in spite of adherence to this pale Belgravian colouring throughout, the effect of twenty years' building by about sixteen different architects was of single separate mansions rather than the controlled variety of the Park Villages. Many an American neighbourhood of elderly elephantine houses, packed in mature greenery earlier in this century, had something of the air of Kensington Palace Gardens, whatever the differences of materials, porches, and so on.

So this eminent Kensington collection sometimes called Million-aires' Row accumulated, not so closely packed or so uniform as the Pembridge Gardens of London, but with a density of houses among the trees and shrubberies and gas lamps on either side of its wide avenue comparable to the not quite so elephantine villas for large merchants with large families on Tulse Hill, say, in the suburbs of South London. Yet Kensington Palace Gardens, more grand and more central, had a slightly more complicated ancestry and perhaps a more numerous progeny. Today, with its embassies and the gates at both ends, it is a private road that has suffered little of the social change of Tulse Hill with its blocks of modern flats.

Much of the planting of Mid-Victorian inner suburban London

is still with us, as a walk in May in Kensington or near Wandsworth Common will show: 'rhododendron, chestnut, lilac, Portugal laurel, weeping lime, laburnum, and may', the auctioneer's catalogue reeled them off when established property came up for sale. Said one more sanguine than the rest: 'The luxuriant shrubberies and plantations that encircle it keep the cold winds at a most respectable distance.' 'A little Elysium' was this auctioneer's favourite description: 'Longevity prevails on this healthy property.' Many Mid-Victorian gardens still had a post-Repton picturesqueness of layout, but a vogue for formal terraces of carpet-bedding was encouraged by Paxton's garden layout for the Sydenham Crystal Palace, by Barry's country house landscaping, and by the geometrical garden designs of William Andrews Nesfield—all influenced by Italian formal gardens.

The conservatory became indispensable wherever there was room for it, if only a fernery in a Wardian case on the landing. There was an astonishing, and at the time, solely British vogue for ferns— growing them, drawing them, collecting them dried in herbaria, displaying them in great bowls in drawing rooms, reading and writing handbooks about them—a vogue soon reflected in the United States, but not so much on the Continent. Fern literature flourished, including a multi-volume *Species Filicum* by Sir William Jackson Hooker of Kew, several books ranging from a 'magnificent folio' to a 'handy little volume' by Thomas Moore of the Chelsea Botanic Garden, a history of British ferns by Edward Newman, a popular work by Anne Pratt, a compendious *Geographical Handbook of All Known Ferns*, many of these books with coloured illustrations by chromolithography or wood engraving. Ferns were a prelude to the taste for exotic-leaved indoor plants that was to gather force in the Sixties. Ferns also bore overtones of fossils and the great tree ferns of the coal strata, familiar to a public with a long-standing taste for geology, the first of the sciences to raise questions about Creation. Lyell's *Principles of Geology* of 1830 had reached a ninth edition by 1853, when his more elementary manual hived off from it in 1838 reached its fourth. A shop in the Strand selling drawing-room ornaments (vases, obelisks, paper-weights) in the Forties had found it profitable to advertise not only 'extensive assortment of Shells, Minerals, Fossils etc.' but also 'private instruction in Mineralogy'.

Ferns, too, were part of a taste for what would popularly now be called 'see-through' materials: fringe, network valances, pierced screens, window tracery. Part, too, of an intense interest in the uses of natural foliage in the architectural arts. During 1857–8 in the profession, faithfully reported in the journals, papers on architectural foliage fell like autumn leaves. Gilbert Scott lecturing at the Royal Academy, Street and Seddon and Brandon and Scott at the Architectural Museum (by then at South Kensington) contradicted by Colling and Kerr at the Institute of British Architects, Dresser in the *Art Journal* on botany as adapted to art-manufacture, earnest conjectures by the growing army of Ruskin-readers on the proper relation between art and science, and of both to natural and revealed religion, Ruskin himself on the new carvings at the Oxford Museum, Owen Jones's *Grammar of Ornament* with its plates on natural leaves. Fashionable young journalists of the 1970s like to see all this foliage concern as 'proto-Art Nouveau', an anachronism. For it was completely of its time. One outcome was to be the extraordinary vegetation applied to the Grosvenor Hotel at Victoria Station (next chapter).

The successful hotel of the Fifties was the Great Western Hotel at Paddington Station (*Fig. 18*), opened in 1852, the first of the breed that Disraeli (in *Lothair*) was to call 'bran-new brobdignagian hotel'; in fact, when the Grosvenor was first mooted in October 1858, it was to be 'an imitation' of the Great Western, which, 'owing to its large profits, is uniformly quoted by joint-stock hotel promoters' ('Money Market and City Intelligence', *The Times*). The Great Western, designed by the eclectic architect Philip Charles Hardwick, who had already carried on his father's work at Euston which included two small hotels, was indeed the pioneer of mid-century 'monster' railway hotels in London, with its mansard roofs and prominent towers, suites of rooms for families, and profitable returns. Stucco was still fashionable in commercial circles when it was built. It made the older hotels such as Mivart's (Claridge's), in a series of altered Georgian houses, and even Morley's in Trafalgar Square, look small.

Paddington Station itself was just being built under Brunel, combining curved roofspans of glass and iron with architectural flourishes, such as the station master's oriel window, applied by Matthew Digby Wyatt—a new programme of calling in the art-man after the engineer had made the basic decisions, and then inducing or allowing hotel promoters to commission another architect, Hardwick, to drape a hotel in front of the slightly decorated train sheds. Lewis Cubitt's King's Cross Station, then just finished, was the last station complex—shed, frontispiece, hotel on the side— designed entirely by one man. This was not the case at Euston,

Fig. 18 *Great Western Hotel, Paddington*

where the station had been designed by Robert Stephenson. The
contractors at Euston, both for railway construction and for building
Hardwick Sr's grand frontispiece, had been the firm of William
Cubitt when his brother Lewis was a partner, hence the latter's
experience in these matters. At King's Cross, the double-arched
screen expressing the dual shed behind was a refinement of the
architectural screen Lewis Cubitt had designed for Bricklayers'
Arms Station. While Paddington Station was reared at the edge of
several newly developed residential areas, King's Cross rose in a
fringe area between estates to southward ranging from dignified
gentility (Bedford Estate) to slum pockets among lesser gentility

71

(Foundling Estate, Gray's Inn Road area), and the suburban Sahara to northward that lay across the paths of City clerks walking home to Holloway (long before the Pooters): that tract 'where tiles and bricks were burnt, bones were boiled, carpets were beat, rubbish was shot, dogs were fought, and dust was heaped by contractors . . . [and] the light of its kiln fires made lurid smears on the fog' (*Our Mutual Friend*). Yet memories varied, and the fields varied. The *Builder* in 1865, contemplating new suburban trains passing over the North London Railway viaduct, filled with thousands 'carpet-bags in hand' being borne toward Broad Street Station, remembered 'the solitude which once reigned . . . the quiet nooks', and sheep and cattle browsing in Copenhagen Fields a few years before.

Among notable public buildings opened or begun in the Fifties were two by the Government architect Pennethorne. The Museum of Practical Geology was built during 1845–9 and opened in 1851 to house the Geological Survey and collections begun in Craig's Court, Whitehall, in 1837. Entered from Jermyn Street on a site running through to Piccadilly (now occupied by Simpson's shop), the museum was a dignified warm-hued stone *palazzo* outside with well-planned gallery spaces, only too soon outgrown, inside. The Public Record Office, begun on Fetter Lane in 1851, grew slowly, 'in the Anglo-Saxon manner' as some cynic put it, until the Sixties (extended to Chancery Lane 1891–6). The erection of this building —incidentally letting in some light among the mouldering warrens of the Law, as Dickens in 1852–3 was doing in another sense through the pages of *Bleak House*—at last afforded a home to historic government records previously kept in unsuitable places such as the Chapter House of Westminster Abbey and the Norman chapel in the Tower of London. So Pennethorne rigorously adapted a faintly Gothic style to archives' storage, with a dignified flourish of turrets.

That other haunt of scholars, the British Museum Reading Room (*Fig. 19*), was opened in 1857, Sydney Smirke having filled in his elder brother's useless central quadrangle with a great domed space to take the place of small reading rooms on Montague Place. The dome, technically impressive and the most restful ceiling in the world to work under, was painted light blue picked out in gold as now; a scheme for its decoration prepared by Alfred Stevens came to nothing. The radial lines of desks like the spokes of a wheel were given those comfortable chairs that still seated readers in the 1950s but have since been, alas, replaced.

Nearby, at the corner of New Oxford and Museum Streets,

Fig. 19 *British Museum Reading Room*

Fig. 20 *Mudie's Library: a literary party in 1860*

Mudie's circulating library catered to less scholarly tastes with a success marked by the gala party opening its new be-galleried, be-columned hall in 1860 (*Fig. 20*). And on railway station platforms there were, increasingly, the bookstalls of W. H. Smith & Son, so careful of the moral tone of railway reading. Henry James later described 'the fine flare of one of Mr W. H. Smith's bookstalls' on the foggy platform of St Pancras or King's Cross in the Eighties, 'a focus of warmth and light in the vast smoky cavern', giving the idea that literature was 'a thing of splendour . . . of infinite gas-lit red and gold'.

The British Museum, then as now, was the instructive place to take the children. The Ethnographical Rooms, for instance (today in Burlington Gardens): 'You have now seen the evidence of heathenism abroad,—come and see that of Britain. . . .' 'Oh, aunt,' said Lucy, 'I can hardly fancy heathenism in Britain' (*Pleasant Mornings in the British Museum, c.* 1857).

Nevertheless, the heathen forms of Islamic Cairo shaped another home of (briefly) improving instruction, the Royal Panopticon of Science and Art on the east side of Leicester Square (on the site of some eighteenth-century houses, one by James Gibbs used after 1800 as a hotel). When the Panopticon, designed by T. Hayter Lewis, opened in 1854, it had a stuccoed front incorporating Minton tiles, a pair of minarets, and a conical roof over a large rotunda. Originally there was intended a huge ridge-and-furrow glass dome, technically inspired by the Crystal Palace with a somewhat onion-shaped contour 'taken from a daguerreotype of a dome in Cairo', but the site had no space for buttressing it. Improving instruction did not pay in Leicester Square, and in 1858 this became the Alhambra, music hall and variety theatre extraordinary (*Fig. 38* and Chapter 6).

Owen Jones now added something of the original Alhambra in Spain to the decoration of St James's Hall, opened in 1858 on part of the future site of the Piccadilly Hotel, and accommodating for over forty years, with its fine acoustics and uncomfortable seats, everything from the Monday Pops and the Moore & Burgess Minstrels to meetings addressed by Mr Gladstone. Orientalisms of various sorts were in the air: the *Illustrated London News*'s first colour plates, made by a wood-engraving process, included views of India during that period of intense interest in India of the Mutiny and the last days of the East India Company. A pair of bandstands set up in the Royal Horticultural Gardens in Kensington,

laid out during 1859–61 by Nesfield the garden designer, roman-
tically reflected the roof forms of Indian pavilions like delayed
reflections of the Brighton Pavilion. One of these band pavilions
still stands on Clapham Common.

Roofs were in the news during the five-year controversy over
new buildings for Government offices in Whitehall south of Downing Street. The architectural competition held in 1856 became an
arena not only for that professional disagreement known as the
Battle of the Styles (Gothic *v*. Classic, and both *v*. modern French
influence from the New Louvre), but also for the opinions of
politicians and the interference of the Prime Minister. Victorian
architectural competitions were quite often the most unprofessional
affairs imaginable, yet it has been the curious vindication of many
such cases of muddling through that the buildings emerging in
spite of them have been so good. Following the Royal Exchange
competition of 1838, the Great Exhibition and Government Offices
competitions of the Fifties, and the Law Courts competition of the
Sixties, not one of the resulting structures was built by the winner
of the competition concerned. That the Home, Foreign, and
Colonial Offices finally begun in the Sixties were not built in High
Victorian Gothic or in high-roofed Second Empire, or even with
Barry's high domes, we owe to that Late Georgian, Lord Palmerston.
Gilbert Scott's Italian palace, as seen from St James's Park with its
tower picturesquely set off by a rounded wing (*Fig. 21*), suggests
that Scott had seen the original or an engraving of Claude Lorrain's
popular painting *The Enchanted Castle*, which had been in England
for many years (exhibited at the British Institution in Pall Mall in
1851) and which then belonged to a Manchester banker S. J. Loyd,
who became Lord Overstone. Perhaps that has not been suggested
before. Scott's building in its large-scale all-over ornament and
assertiveness was a product of the Sixties. The other designs that
'placed' in the competition had a paper life of their own from being
so prominently exhibited and published and argued about; some
were influential outside London.

Meanwhile, William Burn, a skilled and sensible country house
architect who was one of the assessors in the competition, calmly
designed steep French roofs for Montagu House (1859–62) on the
other side of Whitehall, and Thomas Cundy II subsequently followed suit on the Grosvenor Estate. But steep roofs had appeared in
London (well before the New Louvre vogue) on the Houses of
Parliament, a building entirely out of fashion among the new Gothic

75

Fig. 21 *The Foreign Office, from St James's Park*

men long before it was finished. That roof slant behind the pinnacles and parapets loomed out of the river mists in the spirit of the Gothic north, fit neighbour to the steep-roofed Abbey. The unbuilt Gothic designs on Whitehall, bristling and polychromatic, would have been fit neighbour to neither.

In the background of all this architectural fussing, up and down Whitehall and in the House of Commons, fumed the River. Insistently fumed the Thames, miles of it, as the sewage of a population nearing three millions of people, with all the wastes of factories, breweries and chemical works, flowed into it. Philosophers rejoiced that it flowed right under Parliament's 'own wise nose' (Peacock writing *Gryll Grange* in 1859) and the *Builder* worried over London's insufficient 'knowledge on the subject of deodorizing'. Since the cholera epidemic of 1848–9 the subject had been much in the air in more than one sense, and the hot dry summer of 1858 presented the issue more offensively than ever, creating 'as much anxiety in the public mind as did the revolt in India of last year' (*Clapham Gazette*). During the summer of 1859 every newspaper ran leaders on the state of the Thames.

A Metropolitan Board of Works had been appointed under the Local Management Act of 1855, with one of its principal responsibilities the main drainage of London, to which end a further Act was passed in 1858. The plan was to make two sets of 'intercepting sewers', one north and one south of the Thames and parallel to it, to take the flow down to Barking and Crossness for treatment before discharge into the river many miles below London Bridge. This plan in all its ramifications took some years to complete (next chapter). Meanwhile sheets soaked in chloride of lime hung across Parliament's riverside windows. The already foetid courtyards of the poor near the Strand, and the great segment of South London partly encircled by the poisoned river, also faced the prevailing south-westerly winds that have always caused the Metropolis to grow westward, away from windborne urban smells. (Still today, Londoners living to eastward of a brewery—a by no means wholly unpleasant smell—know all about prevailing winds.) For some writers on the Victorian Age, the Fifties were a golden time: it depended where you sat.

The continual forces of migration within and into the Metropolis never ceased. The more offices, shops, warehouses were rebuilt or enlarged in the centre, the more trains, omnibuses, steamboats and the incomes to afford private carriages increased to make suburban life possible; the more the better-off residents of central London moved out to the widening periphery, the more the multiplying poor and new migrants from the provinces moved into leftover central premises or the courtyards behind them. At all levels the magnet Metropolis continued to attract multitudes seeking work or fame or charity or whatever might turn up at the end of the rainbow.

Very gradually, the conditions of life for many people did begin to improve. So far as the fabric of London was concerned, there was more money for both private and public building. The District Boards of Works appointed in 1855 started to tackle local drainage and other local improvements. And by dint of the private and public efforts of individuals with energy, imagination and good will, there was a gradual increase in that 'regard for human life that attends civilisation' (the Registrar General on the Census of 1861, quoted by Jephson). Or so it seemed.

In 1859 the church of All Saints, Margaret Street, east of upper Regent Street between Great Titchfield and Wells Streets, was consecrated after ten years of building and decoration. It was the first and perhaps one of the finest examples in Victorian England of 'structural colour', the banding of one material with another, red bricks with black outside, marbles and granites, glazed bricks and alabaster inside, in a sort of geological layering. The architect was William Butterfield, the builder was John Kelk, and both money and ideas were supplied by Alexander James Beresford Hope, the High Gothic son of the connoisseur Thomas Hope.

Also in 1859, among the jostlings of large issues and the publication of great books (*The Origin of Species*, *On Liberty*, *Self-Help*), there was one small departure. Vauxhall Gardens (founded in the eighteenth century), after bowing off many times like an ageing opera star, put on its final fireworks display, 'Farewell Forever', and closed. Even before the railway embankment from Nine Elms to Waterloo ran alongside the Gardens, its lamp-lit outdoor entertainments had attracted roughs as well as rain (the high-toned winter garden at Sydenham felt safe from such risks). In the Forties the French showman-conductor M. Jullien had conducted there with all his panache, although the attempt by his fellow-Parisian M. Musard to revive Vauxhall's 'dying glories' with masquerades had been spoilt by riotous vulgarity among the guests. Yet Dickens saw the Duke of Wellington there in 1849, watching a performance of the Battle of Waterloo. The baroque bravura of its firework displays on summer nights had supplied something London lacked before great fountains and fireworks arrived at Sydenham. This lack was especially felt after the weak debut of the Trafalgar Square fountains —each platter with its slender gush of water like a coachman's whip, unlike the better managed sprays today. Some people agreed with Professor Cockerell's irritable remarks in 1842 at the Royal Academy (then overlooking the Square) that 'our aqueducts are from Heaven—we have more than enough in a country of umbrellas', fountains in England were 'pure Pedantry—a mere servile Imitation of Rome and Paris, and contrary to the Genius of our country and habits'. Nevertheless, some years before the début of fountains at Sydenham, Prince Albert had thought differently.

In 1849, under his direction Nesfield the garden designer produced some drawings for landscaping the space between Buckingham Palace and Green Park (where the Victoria Memorial was placed after 1901) with a set of grandiose fountains expressing just the sort of Victorianized baroque heroics so liked by the London public in loyal allegories at Vauxhall: Britannia on the Apex of a Rock directing Plenty to diffuse her Gifts over the Globe, which Rests on the Shoulders of Atlas attended by Commerce and Neptune, all for casting in bronze and granite at the centre of a 425-foot pool with swan fountains at both ends (unexecuted drawing in RIBA Drawings Collection). Nesfield probably meant his design to simulate the Piazza Navona at Rome when that was flooded like a lake for a festival, as drawn by Piranesi, with Bernini's fountain in the centre—but it was really more like Vauxhall Gardens:

> . . . you expect every minute to see the fireworks spring up into the air, and make sure that the Genius of Britannia, holding a medallion of the Royal Family on the tip of her trident, will presently advance . . . whilst Jullien [Commerce and Neptune in one?] directs an explosive crash of music that subsides as soon as the Roman candles are nearly burnt out, into a cry of 'Hats off', and a soft bar of 'God Save the Queen'. (*Punch*, 26 August 1848)

In the summer of 1860 the foundation stone for a quite different institution was laid on part of the Vauxhall Gardens site: a group of schools including a Lambeth School of Art behind the site of an impending church of St Peter (next chapter), both designed by John Loughborough Pearson. (The vicarage is the altered Georgian house of the Gardens' manager.) An evening drawing school, said to provide London's first art classes for artisans—pottery, engineering and building workers of the parish—had been founded in other premises in 1854 by the parson of St Mary's, Lambeth, in connection with the Government school of design at Marlborough House. It trained painters and modellers for Messrs Doulton's pottery works nearby on the riverbank, and decorative carvers who took their skills to many masons' yards; some were to be sculptors on Scott's Government office building in Whitehall, and some went for further training to the Royal Academy Schools. The stone-laying in June 1860 was the first such ceremony ever performed by the Prince of Wales, attended by various dignitaries including the energetic Henry Cole. Children's schools nearer the church were finished by another architect in 1868. A little to the south-east, cricket had been played at the Oval since 1845.

The end of the Early Victorian era can be said to have occurred (if any one day can be said to mark the end of an era) on 22 May 1860. This was the day of Sir Charles Barry's funeral in Westminster Abbey, the day on which he had hoped to crown with the Royal standard the finally completed Victoria Tower, London's first and, for about a century after its first design in 1835, only monumental tower on that scale until the Senate House of the University of London was built.

CHAPTER FOUR

The Sixties: Tidal London

The London theme of the Sixties, it could be said, was tidal: the river, the sewers, the roads, the railways, the food markets, the money market, and all the machinery of flux in human existence needed drastic treatment during this decade when the metropolitan population approached three millions. A German visitor to the 1851 Exhibition, commenting fearfully on 'the world-city of the present age', had thought that 'things have been conducted here to the *utmost limits* of the present social system' and that 'some novel, unexpected change or revulsion' must be at hand. 'Can anyone think that we will say, *anno* 1860 or 1870, London has now three millions of people, and so on *ad infinitum* . . . I do not speak politics . . . [yet] the thought of "*anne ultra?*" struck my mind . . . we stand on the threshold of some great social crisis.' With that 'certain quiet *aplomb* and steadiness' which he noted in the national character, the Londoners who wondered 'what about next year?' pressed slowly on with whatever had occurred to them to do about it.

French visitors during the Exhibition year of 1862 complained of the *tumulte formidable* of London's crowded streets (complained too that people spoke English all day long, 'and all the syllables seem to arise and die in the throat'). There was 'vast burrowing' for the new Underground Railway and the new sewers, with 'obstructive sheds under whose roofs gravel and clay rise to the surface', 'a huge and hideous contrivance, resembling most a monstrous packing-case, being fixed across one and another broad thoroughfare' (*Companion to the British Almanac* for 1863 and 1864). Moreover, the 'drastic nature' of the new drainage measures temporarily caused more typhus in neighbourhoods where the great intercepting sewer was in process of construction in 1864. Architects were having

their troubles, with all the best bricks and cement going underground, yet the meticulous sewer brickwork was to provide a new
standard for the modern-minded and practical: the new Outfall
Sewer was 'faced inside with bricks of the hardest and best kind, and
laid with a degree of care and finish that a few years ago would have
been thought unnecessary on the exterior of a mansion' (*Companion
to the Almanac for 1863*). And by means of the new Underground
Railway and new suburban lines, a London architect might visit
more sites and more clients in a professional day than before. In the
early Forties, the architect of a new town, Kingston-on-Railway
(Surbiton), drove smartly down to the site from London in his four-
in-hand (that was Stevens of Stevens & Alexander, before Coutts
Bank foreclosed his client's mortgage and replaced him by P. C.
Hardwick). But a phenomenon like Gilbert Scott, who between 1847
and 1878 was concerned with about 700 buildings, could never have
occurred in a century without railways; the ground covered by his
cathedral-restoring predecessor James Wyatt in a carriage could be
multiplied many times. It has been conjectured, however, that much
relentless over-restoration of country churches may have gone on
because busy London architects didn't take to the railways often
enough to supervise local workmen properly.

Opinions about railways depended on one's generation. A young
curate lecturing in 1862 to the Clapham Literary and Scientific
Institution, observed the lines near Clapham Junction, where 'you
will see at least half a dozen trains, some up, some down, some
across, some over, some under, rushing about here and there like
comets', and thought it was all 'in strict accordance and harmony
with the progressive wants of society'. Unlike old Benjamin Cooper,
who lived in the Wandsworth Road, overlooking new railway viaducts across Battersea Fields, just before his death aged 95 (*Clapham
Gazette*, July 1865), and who considered it wrong to travel in a
carriage without horses, being fond of telling about a friend of his
who had to go from York to London: 'as there were no longer any
coaches he acted like a man . . . why, he walked.'

In the summer of 1863, there was a mass visit by members of
local Boards of Works from all over the Metropolis to the new Main
Drainage Outfall at Barking, where about a thousand of them sat
down to dinner in the bed of the new reservoir, including a man
who said 'things had gone on very well before and we were doing a
great deal of harm in meddling with them' (*Clapham Gazette*,
August 1863). His point of view persisted in 'the lamentation of the

G

Prologue of the Westminster [School] play over the drying-up of the well in Dean's Yard, which, if sanitary science were as well understood at Westminster as the classics would have figured in the Prologue as a matter of congratulation. . . . Underground railways and main drainage works will indirectly do a deal of good in this way. In our own parish many wells have been dried up by the new sewers, much to the welfare and dissatisfaction of the inhabitants,' said the clear-eyed editor of the *Clapham Gazette*, George Meaden, in January 1866. Since Meaden acted as chairman of the Wandsworth District Board of Works during this purgatorial period, and sat on the Metropolitan Board as well, he knew what separating the drains from the water supply meant.

Yet local authorities remained deeply conscious of their limitations. In 1863 a discussion took place at a meeting of the Wandsworth District Board of Works, reflecting the constant tug-of-war behind the scenes between well-meaning men. The subject of their discourse was the open Heathwall Ditch. Open to the tidal Thames at both ends, open to the sky, it skirted the south edge of the still marshy meadows of Battersea Fields at the foot of steep little streets running down from the old road to Kingston (Wandsworth Road and Lavender Hill), the road itself skirting further rising ground covered with new building developments and their new drains. The Heathwall Ditch was about to become part of the Southern Low Level Sewer system, but until that happened some slowness in leasing, for instance of new villas in Cedars Road, was doubtless due to 'dreadful effluvium' borne along on the wind. Westward, the upper part of Lavender Hill with its eighteenth-century villas may have been high enough to look down its nose, but eastward along the Wandsworth Road, modest ribbon-development rows of little houses were all too near the ditch. The District Board in November 1863 was discussing a butcher's shop on the bank of the Heathwall, where meat went bad three hours after its arrival in the shop: 'Mr Greenwood said that the state of Battersea Fields was a disgrace to the Board. . . . The Chairman did not see how the Board could interfere . . . Mr Greenwood argued that it was the duty of the Board to prevent houses being in such places. . . . Mr Tolcher was as ardent a sanitary reformer as any member of the Board, but the Board had no power of interfering where people should build houses, as it would be said they were interfering with private rights', and so on.

Private rights in the building of new houses, slightly tempered under the Metropolitan Building Act of 1855 with regard to party-wall construction and the prevention of eaves-dripping on the public way, were to be further supervised under a series of Acts on the building of artisans' dwellings, and a series of Acts extending the powers of local authorities to deal with existing sanitary 'nuisances'. ('Nuisances', that official catch-all word, like 'incidents' in wartime.) All of this legislation, according to an experienced solicitor testifying before a Royal Commission on the housing of the poor in 1884–5, was about as complicated as the Church Building Acts, 'which nobody has as yet understood' (quoted by R. A. Cross, Disraeli's Home Secretary, on the housing Acts of 1875 and 1879, in the *Nineteenth Century*, June 1885). The immediate problem was that borderland of action between a metropolitan body and local bodies, the row over who paid to clean up the more notorious nuisances. Meanwhile, main drainage construction went on and was royally declared open in 1865, although much then remained to be done.

Certain features of the main drainage system had a surprising architecture, regarded as one of the Lions of London all during the century. At first the elaborate interiors of the pumping stations at Crossness (1865) and Abbey Mills (1868) shocked 'the ordinary vestry mind'. 'Why, sir,' said one bewildered district-board-of-works member of the latter, 'the building might be taken for a Turkish mosque or a Chinese temple . . . no music-hall in London can be compared with it' (*Companion to the British Almanac for 1869*). Who would ever go there? Yet, still in the Eighties, London writers said: 'The Crossness Works are perfectly wonderful . . . nearly all noted foreigners who visit England inspect them' (Cassell's *Greater London*). The Metropolitan Board's chief engineer, Joseph Bazalgette, who superintended their design, knew what he was about. There was something marvellous and utterly new in at last saving the world's largest city from its awful purgatory of the Forties and Fifties. In these two pumping-temples flanking the Thames, there are splendid pillars of indescribably congested style, and flowing ironwork foliage of parapet and tympanum screens, combined with the technical splendours of great beam-engines to impress the marvellous fact as no existing architectural style, tied to existing building types, could. (Tours of the main drainage pumping stations can sometimes be arranged through the department of public health engineering of the Greater London Council.)

Bazalgette's other great work, for which he was knighted in 1874, was the embanking of the Thames, that is, turning the old straggling congeries of wharves, coal barges and mud into a series of urban quays. The London Museum has several views showing (rather too neatly) what Thames-shore life 150 yards below the Strand was like before Bazalgette: from William Marlow's painting of the 1770s while the Adelphi was being built to John O'Connor's painting of a century later (in retrospect of a few years before), showing mud-flats littered with boatyard debris or high tide slapping at crazy old shacks and wharfside taverns. Ancient steep lanes ran down from the Strand. Carting Lane opposite Southampton Street, now daylit and prosaic between the Savoy Hotel and Shell-Mex House, was one of these; Ivybridge Lane was another, on the west side of Shell-Mex (formerly Hotel Cecil). In the Forties, you found the dark entry to Ivybridge Lane beside a clock shop in the Strand and plunged down the lane's gloomy length with the 'horrid vaulted maze' of the Adelphi Arches on your right—that mysterious sub-structure of the Adelphi half-lit by the 'Rembrandtish' firelight of wretched 'metropolitan outcasts' who lived there—and you emerged on the smelly shore where a 'mite of a public-house propped . . . on stilts out of the river mud' called the Fox-under-the-Hill leaned beside the ha'penny-steamboat pier (*Builder*, 'London strolls', 1857, and James Greenwood, 'The boat of all-work', collected in his *Unsentimental Journeys, or Byways of the Modern Babylon*, 1867, but harking back to the Forties when this was the ramshackle landing stage for ramshackle boats used by the poorest costermongers between Hungerford or Covent Garden markets and a pier near Billingsgate, until one boat, the *Cricket*, blew up at this pier in August 1847). O'Connor's view suggests the limbo of shacks and wharves still clustering at the hem of the Adelphi Arches just before the Victoria Embankment was begun. Our photograph of about 1900 (*Fig. 51*) taken from an upper window of the Adelphi beside the Hotel Cecil shows, below, the remains of Ivybridge Lane at the old limit of high tide and, in front, the Embankment Gardens created on the site of the Fox-under-the-Hill and the poor man's pier.

The Victoria Embankment from Westminster to Blackfriars was sanctioned by Parliament in 1862; complicated by the two construc-tions for low-level sewer and underground railway, it took until 1870 to finish. The Albert Embankment, on the south side of the river from Vauxhall Bridge to Westminster Bridge, was sanctioned in 1863 and completed in 1869. Then, Millbank to Chelsea having been completed in the early Fifties, the Chelsea Embankment from

Battersea Bridge to Chelsea Bridge, sanctioned in 1858, was finished in 1874, as also was the spider's-web Gothic Albert Bridge built in connection with it, to the design of the engineer R. M. Ordish (*Fig. 34*). The Albert Bridge must have been partly inspired by the jungle of ships' rigging further downriver. Sophisticated as the ornaments of urban quays should be are the cast iron coiling-dolphin lamp standards and, on Victoria Embankment, the benches with crouching camels and sphinxes, apparently added when Cleopatra's Needle was installed (next chapter) and in honour of the British takeover of the Suez Canal. As for the giant blocks of fine masonry forming the river wall itself, commentators at the end of the Sixties were rightly pleased at such 'largeness and breadth of style . . . quite refreshing to look upon, in these days of niggle and minutiae', 'probably the finest piece of granite-work in London' (the annual architectural criticism in the *Companion to the British Almanac* could be sharp, so this was praise indeed). Studding the Westminster embankment wall, well above normal high-tide level, are bronze lion-heads biting large mooring rings fit to hold Venetian argosies while some stove-pipe-hatted doge celebrates his Marriage with the Thames. (If 'the lions are drinking', their Council masters still say, the Thames is in flood.) Bazalgette knew when grandeur must be simple. There is a memorial to him on the Embankment opposite the foot of Northumberland Avenue (for that new street, see next chapter). He was later responsible for bridges at Putney, Battersea, and Hammersmith (where he was somewhat carried away by the idea of huge volutes expressing the energy of suspension chains) and for the Woolwich Free Ferry (instead of a bridge where the river is so wide and deep-sea ships so large). Any foot passenger who rode that ferry in its last days in the 1950s will remember the freedom to patrol its wide-open deck and inspect passing liners being tugged to the Royal Docks, and the chance to stroll past the ferry's engine-room while the engineer chased urchins from its pounding machinery; in contrast to the segregation, as of cattle, below-decks practised on pedestrians using the new ferries today (in the interests of the motor-cars on deck above), hardly worth a free ride. (A Ride with a View is this book's motto.) The old ferries, waddling and crab-shaped with tall smoke-stacks, performed heroic rescue work during the bombing of the docks in the Second World War.

New Thames bridges of the Sixties included the Alexandra (or Cannon Street Railway) Bridge, supported by huge hemi-semi-Doric iron columns; Blackfriars, ornamented with squat Gothic columns, and its neighbouring railway bridge, of which pair some critics observed that at least each partly hid the other; the Hungerford (Charing Cross) rail and foot bridge, replacing the old pedestrian suspension bridge, its chains going to Clifton; a new Westminster Bridge to replace the first bridge built upstream from Old London Bridge, and with trefoil parapet to suit the Houses of Parliament; the first Lambeth Bridge to replace the Archbishop of Canterbury's anything-but-free ferry; the Grosvenor Railway Bridge to Victoria Station (begun in 1859 near Chelsea Bridge, which was finished in 1858); and the Wandsworth (or Battersea) Railway Bridge to Kensington and a link with the Great Western lines from Padding-ton. With trains crossing at Blackfriars enabled to link up with lines at King's Cross (later in this chapter), London was completely encircled by railways and these were further enmeshed with the half-underground, half-in-the-open Metropolitan and Metro-politan District Lines (Circle and District and Metropolitan Lines today). The seven-mile hank of river from Putney to the City had been crossed in 1837 by eight bridges, five of the eighteenth century and three of the early nineteenth. To these the Forties added one foot bridge and the Fifties one road bridge and the beginnings of a railway bridge, whereas the Sixties added not only one new road bridge and two replacements, but the five railway bridges. Here came the first railways to cross the river, as in central Paris they never did. Henry James in 1877, on his way by boat from West-minster to Greenwich, looked up as they passed under 'the dark hugely piled bridges, where the railway trains and the human pro-cessions' were forever moving, and thought that the 'tremendous piers of the bridges' seemed 'the very pillars of the Empire'.

There are many oddities of road layout in relation to the river, a large tongue of South London being partly enclosed by the Thames reaches regarded by north-of-the-river as belonging peculiarly to Westminster, the Strand, and the City. On this tongue of Southwark and Lambeth are a number of road intersections or hubs that the French would call *rond-points*, but having nothing to do with influence from Haussmann's Paris, being dictated by the wheel-spoke layout of roads from the Thames bridges. For example, London's first two bridges were approximately perpendicular to one another. Now, roads from Lambeth, Westminster, Waterloo, Blackfriars, Southwark and London bridges, as well as ancient roads southward and to Dover, all converge, with some local irregularity, on or near the old hub at Elephant and Castle. There is a more planned convergence at St George's Circus, designed in the eighteenth century by George Dance the Younger for roads from the first Blackfriars and Westminster bridges and the Lambeth ferry. When old Riah in *Our Mutual Friend* walked from St Mary Axe to Westminster to see Jenny Wren, he left the City by London Bridge and took a road skirting the south shore to Westminster Bridge as the quickest route, on a shorter radius than the way via Fleet Street, Strand, and Whitehall.

In fact, if we look at any present-day map of London, we find that the northward twist of the river between Greenwich and Nine Elms presents the surprising but undeniable situation that Waterloo Station is north of Buckingham Palace, Bankside is north of the Ritz, London Bridge Station is north of Hyde Park Corner and very much north of Victoria Station, which lies in the same latitude as Elephant and Castle, and so on. 'North' versus 'south' of the river has always been a state of mind, rather than of the map, induced by the one-sided situation of power (until County Hall was built on the South Bank) and the history of an alluvial flood-plain long devoted to market gardens. The first north-of-the-river sneer must have curled the lips of Londinium Romans, looking over their shoulders at their first suburb (Southwark) clustering disreputably at the other end of their wooden bridge. Thus Romans at home about Trastevere, thus Florentines about the Oltr'Arno ('the shady part of the town,' said Augustus Hare). Thus mankind wherever it settles beside a natural boundary.

In 1862 the Roupell forgery case was inciting north-of-the-river newspaper sneers at the whole transpontine world from Deptford to Battersea, as a 'dingy, dubious, debatable land . . . desperately cheap and desperately nasty' with 'an indescribable odour of dissent', as the 'second hand' suburban background of Roupell the fraudulent M.P. and landowner 'over the water'. To these aspersions that spirited monthly, the *Clapham Gazette*, acidly inquired whether the fastidious newspaper editor ever visited Clerkenwell or Seven Dials.

The public house that gave its name, the Elephant and Castle, to the busy road junction before it, stood until the Blitz on an island site on the south side between Newington Butts and Walworth Road (the latter is now re-routed, and the Elephant is all rebuilt nearby). For most of the last century the pub was a three-storey Late Georgian affair, 'a mere central starting-point for omnibuses

. . . formerly a well-known coaching house' (Walford, *Old and New London*, c. 1878), but in the Nineties it was flamboyantly enlarged and heightened, with a prominent be-castled elephant among its cupolas (*Fig. 52*). The copper elephant is now set up on the concourse of the new shopping centre; two like him still stand on a Victorian public house beside Vauxhall Station.

On Newington Butts near the Elephant stood the Metropolitan Tabernacle, of which the Corinthian portico remains. It was built in 1859–61 in the manner of a purer and duller Royal Exchange outside, with an iron-columned amphitheatre inside (rebuilt later after a fire), for Charles Haddon Spurgeon, the rousing young preacher who drew people in thousands. The present Ministry of Health site on the Newington Causeway side of the intersection was occupied in 1863 by William Tarn's newly rebuilt five-storey drapery shop, of department store size and watered-down Second Empire lavishness, in this century occupied by Isaac Walton & Co. until the building was bombed in the last war. When Tarn's was opened in 1863, its situation was declared 'not unworthy of being classed as one of the finest in London . . . [with] from morning to night the restlessness of a vast and busy population'. When Pevsner first described the neighbourhood in 1952, it was a 'most unself-conscious muddle of buildings and traffic' and ruins. Today, with the bran-new shopping centre and subways it is less unself-conscious, still a muddle for pedestrians, and bleakly inhuman in scale. In the ebb and flow of its traffic, the Elephant and Castle intersection is still part of the vitals of London.

Such another intersection, at King's Cross, became more complex in the Sixties: its vitality, having begun in the eighteenth century with the traffic of the New Road to Islington and the City, was enhanced in the Fifties by the activities of Caledonian Market and King's Cross Station, to which St Pancras was soon to be added, while to southward the Bedford and Foundling Estates maintained their gates that forced all low, bustling traffic bound for the railway termini or cattle market to use Gray's Inn Road. The road junctions at Victoria and at Charing Cross, too, were to become saturated with traffic generated by new railway termini. Road problems, in fact, were to be more and more bound up with the railways, now entering the heart of London.

A 'Proposed Great Central West-end Terminus', according to some promoter's prose quoted by *The Times* in 1857 (August 27), was to 'purge and cleanse the dirty parts of Pimlico, relieve the

monstrous aggravation of traffic which for years has made London-
bridge a nuisance, make the lonely neighbourhood of Victoria-street
one of the most important sub-centres in the metropolis . . . creating
a grand western centre immediately under the walls of Buckingham
Palace . . . multitudes of visitors bound west of Temple-bar . . .
avoiding altogether the tedious and perilous passes of the City.' To
do this, the Grosvenor Basin with its wharves and yards let to
builders or timber and coal merchants by the former landowner, the
Marquis of Westminister, was to be filled in for the station site, and
most of the canal linking it to the river filled in for the railway lines
coming in over a new Thames bridge. A public house called the
Grosvenor Basin stood until recently in Wilton Road on what had
been the old dock's former east bank, opposite the Hudson's Place
entrance to Victoria Station. The original Grosvenor Basin was a
busy backwater similar in character to the remains of Paddington
Basin today (off Praed Street), and dependent on what was then as
for centuries a chief carrier of London building materials, the
Thames sailing-barge—that workhorse of the river with its burnt-
sienna coloured sails, sails often lettered with advertising like mobile
billboards.

The Victoria and Pimlico Railway Act of 1858 was promoted by
a varied lot of people including a recently risen builder and speculator already mentioned, an M.P. who happened to be a partner in
a firm of lime and cement merchants in Kent, two esquires of no
obvious connections, and a lieutenant-colonel of the East India
Company apparently related to the solicitors piloting the Bill: a
firm of solicitors founded in the eighteenth century and existing
today, of which one brother during his lifetime was an acquaintance
of Keats, a friend of Thackeray, and the oldest living founder of the
Garrick Club, while the other brother was for many years' secretary
to the committee of Drury Lane Theatre—part of the splendidly
motley roots of Victoria Station. In a worldly sense, the ultimately
grandest person (possibly even grander than John Fowler the Chief
Engineer) connected with the making of Victoria Station was John
Kelk the building contractor, who built station, bridge, and also
the Grosvenor Hotel (promoted by a separate company and separate
from the station, where a hotel integrated with the terminus had
been abortively planned). Kelk acquired for himself Bentley Priory
at Stanmore, where Dowager Queen Adelaide had spent some of her
declining years, for his country house and built himself a town
house in Grosvenor Square (middle of east side), sat as M.P. for

Fig. 22 *Victoria Station before 1898*

Harwich 1865–8, was painted by Millais in 1870, and ended up as a baronet (see Albert Memorial, below). The complexity of creating a terminus for several quarrelling companies at Victoria and connecting it with the opposite side of the river was not reflected in the initial station buildings, for example the modest frontage remaining on Hudson's Place, where foreign royalties still arrive and incongruously review troops drawn up in that awkward cul-de-sac. The main forecourt looked like nothing at all (*Fig. 22*) until additions were made in 1898 and 1908.

The only spirited building remaining with any sort of sooty dignity from the Sixties there is the Grosvenor Hotel at one side (rear *Fig. 22*; *Fig. 56*). Its design was compiled by the two Knowleses out of various influences absorbed from the elder's Early Victorian practice and admiration for Barry, with some of the patterns proposed for Whitehall grafted on to Hardwick's patterns on the hotel at Paddington, and from the younger's quick ear for the architectural foliage furore and his eager reading of Ruskin, so that they patterned its walls with 'the oak, the ivy, and the rose'. (Perhaps the American architect Louis Sullivan remembered photographs of the Grosvenor's leafy friezes thirty years later when composing the Wainwright Building in St Louis.) The hotel's interior was somewhat altered by the Waterhouse firm in 1900: the middling-grand staircase must originally have had a balustrade of giant ivy leaves continued down from the gallery. If a new Victoria is built, the Grosvenor's unique twinned cupolas and large-scaled end-pavilion cornices would set off the new cliff face better than any modern substitute.

Charing Cross and Cannon Street Station hotels (1864–6) were both part of the station structure; together with booking halls they masked the riverside trainsheds approached by their new bridges. Some people thought the placing of Charing Cross Station, so near Trafalgar Square, a 'national crime' (Henry James). It was convenient to Carlton House Terrace, where Mr Gladstone lived in 1866. He and his family began their visit to Rome in September by walking over to Charing Cross to catch the Folkestone train. Samuel Butler wrote in the Eighties on the views from Waterloo Bridge, of the 'huge wide-opened jaws of those two Behemoths, the Cannon Street and Charing Cross railway stations [could he really see past the train smoke of Blackfriars railway bridge?] . . . See how they belch forth puffing trains as the breath of their nostrils, gorging and disgorging incessantly those human atoms whose movement is the life of the city.' The architect concerned with both was Edward M. Barry (he had designed the new Covent Garden Opera House before he was thirty) and one of his younger brothers was resident engineer under John Hawkshaw, the distinguished consulting engineer to the South Eastern Railway in charge of these two extensions. It was probably E. M. Barry who finished things off at Cannon Street with slightly Wren-like little spired-lanterned turrets on the street front and at the river end: he had given a talk on Wren's architecture at the Clapham Athenaeum in 1860 and was well aware of the City churches a few yards away from the station, churches then in danger of destruction by the Diocese of London. Also perhaps he was responsible for the ironwork design once prevalent at Charing Cross and on its bridge, a sort of lozenge pattern possibly based on the elaborate grille in Henry VII's Chapel, all architects who heard Gilbert Scott's earnest lecture on Westminster Abbey late in 1859 being aware of that treasury of sources. 'Let us make *use* of it,' Scott had urged them.

Scott's St Pancras Hotel (1865–72), with W. H. Barlow's great train shed (1863–7) behind it, is one of those buildings that must be used regularly to be understood. We come up the series of stairs from the depths of the world's first underground railway (Paddington to Farringdon Street, 1863) against the morning tide of railway commuters to emerge under the immensity of the glass and iron shed full of light and space where trains and people are reduced to their proper dimensions. Or we trudge up the incline from the Euston Road against the altitude nicely calculated, first, to clear the Regent's Canal (King's Cross trains dip under it), and then to store so many beer barrels under the station platforms. After admiring the clock tower high on the right—on the finely laid brick wall below it some hippy has chalked a complimentary 'Tower-Power!' —we walk under the archway with an iron-girdered bridge-of-sighs lodged in it for the hotel's first floor corridor, and so into the panelled booking office with the echoing shed-cavern beyond. Or we approach it from the Pentonville Road on top of a bus at sunset to see the whole Wagnerian stage set of tower and pinnacles, as in John O'Connor's painting of 1884 at the London Museum. The ground width of the shed (*Fig. 23*), a previously unheard-of 240 feet under one span of roof, was nicely illustrated at the time it was built by a learned bystander's remark that Wren's Monument (to the Great Fire of 1666) could be rolled right down the shed without touching either side. The highest point along the centre, 100 feet above the rails, would have accommodated the street fronts of Victoria Street with room to spare. The slightly pointed arch of the

Fig. 23 *St Pancras Station : the shed*

shed had no Gothic connotation whatever, but was the result of engineering calculations of stress. The Gothic connotations of Scott's building were considerable, although it was not, as is sometimes said, simply his Whitehall design (vetoed by Palmerston) unrolled and dusted off. It was Scott's special Gothic mixture, shaken up again in 1865 with elements principally Italian, Flemish and English, applied to a station-hotel programme with only very recent precedents in London. Using the excuse of Gothic irregularity, he was able to curve some of his hotel rooms forward along the station's carriage drive to the hotel's street entrance, punctuated by a porch. Inside the hotel (now British Rail offices), the baroque flights of the grand staircase are anchored securely with gothicized ironwork, a fine specimen of the operation of that empirical blend, romantic common sense. The best descriptions of this unique building are Professor Simmons's book of 1968 and Sir John Summerson's essay of 1970, but it must be seen to be believed. And, like all grand buildings, not peered at from a motor-car.

Bringing the railways through North London to St Pancras and through South London and across the river to Victoria, Charing Cross and Cannon Street was even exceeded in complexity by the iron knots tying all these and the new underground lines together along the River Fleet while that ancient stream, newly enclosed as the Fleet Sewer, was being bridged by the Holborn Road Viaduct. The London, Chatham & Dover brought its lines across the new railway bridge alongside Blackfriars Bridge and brazenly took a railway viaduct right across Ludgate Hill—much hated at the time as an iron bar across Fleet Street's view of St Paul's— to meet the Metropolitan Railway at Farringdon Street, ultimately with a station on Holborn Viaduct. (Blackfriars Railway Station with its Moorish minarets and gilt-lettered stones naming destinations from Penge to St Petersburg was built in the Seventies.) Second-storey office workers in New Bridge Street could thereafter watch all manner of goods from Kent (small boats and great tree-trunks were noted in the 1950s) sliding by on their way to points north of King's Cross. Lines such as the South London, swinging round from Battersea to Ludgate Hill, whatever the destruction of houses in its wake, did put rail travel to work within easier reach once cheap workmen's tickets were instituted in 1865. But the bumptious greed of railways became a byword in London in the Sixties. 'What the Grand Turk was some years ago, what the Czar is to Russophobists, the Pope to Protestant old women, and the

93

Great Beast to the student of Revelations, the London, Chatham, and Dover has been for several years to the stationary, in-dwelling people of this metropolis. No Londoner has looked at the paper for years without half expecting to see that the London, Chatham, and Dover intended to go through his house, or over it, or under it, or, worse still, just behind it or just before it, or possibly to do both or all these things,' said *The Times* on 12 October 1866. Just like motorways.

The London, Chatham & Dover and the London, Brighton & South Coast railway companies between them made South London development extremely difficult. For example, in 1863–4 the Australia merchant Philip Flower bought seventy acres of Long-hedge Farm in Battersea Fields. Men who had been small boys in the Thirties remembered 'an immense herd of cows' there and still in the early Sixties it was a lonely stretch of meadow and arable around a single farmhouse, crossed by a single muddy track that was the only short-cut between Clapham and the new Battersea Park and Chelsea Bridge. Flower's double purpose was to put through a much-needed road (now Queenstown Road, route of the 137 bus) connecting the bridge approach with Cedars Road leading to Clapham Common, and paying for it, profitably, by laying out an estate of houses along its course—two or three thousand houses, it was airily hoped, to be named Park Town. But in this lonely open space the railways had got in first. There were the London, Chatham & Dover company's 'engine stables' and repair shops newly planted across one corner of the farm (which nevertheless were to provide employment for many future tenants of the estate), and there was the network of several companies' lines that railwaymen call the 'Battersea tangle'. This meant taking the new road under two sets of tracks on a path like the knight's move in chess; and to do it, a Private Bill had to be put through Parliament in 1863 to wrest from the London, Brighton & South Coast one-third of an acre of unused land the company held there. The road-making difficulties were such that fewer than 500 houses (of an ultimate 1,500) were built in the estate's first six years, and almost 100 of those were immediately sacrificed in carcass when the London, Brighton & South Coast, winning in the end, elected to cross all the other lines and the road with a high viaduct of its own. Thousands ride daily between Victoria Station and Clapham Junction, or between Victoria and East Brixton, over the branching high-level lines that began in the destruction, not of old market gardens, but of new houses (*Figs. 24, 25*). The well-

Fig. 24 *Railway viaducts from the air, Battersea Fields*

Fig. 25 *Railway viaduct from the ground, Battersea Fields*

known Doré view of South London published in 1872 could have been partly drawn from impressions of serried Park Town house-backs seen from rocking transit along these smoky viaducts. Their hellish aspect, for us, is gone with steam, though their noise still thunders into every nearby room. The railway companies worsted by individual enterprise in 1863 had a sort of revenge—yet the enterprising individuals themselves lived elsewhere.

The Metropolitan Board of Works was heavily engaged in carving roads through London in the Sixties. One was Garrick Street, a much-needed link with the earlier openings linking Leicester Square, Long Acre, the Strand, and the approaches to Covent Garden Market. Another was Southwark Street, parallel to the river, a cross-link between the southern approaches to three bridges and the Borough Market. Garrick Street was soon lined with portly classical dignity borrowed from Pall Mall (e.g. the Garrick Club), while in Southwark Street patterns jagged or curved were adapted from Gothic styles to the verticality of warehouses. At the Hop Exchange, elongated iron columns and thick grillework made an elaborate screen to that stage between Kent hop-fields and London breweries.

Refugees from demolitions for the various juggernauts in central London were swept back into corners already crowded, as was the case with Victoria Street and the slums around Westminster Abbey. Swarms of children played in empty basement excavations bordered by raw arches (future coal cellars) supporting the little-used new pavements of the street, which had merely divided the 'diseased heart' in half: 'a leprous district is not to be purified in this manner by a Diet of contractors, and the chief result has been to cause more huddling together. While the nightmare street of unlet palaces was waiting for more capital to fill its yawning gulf, and a few more residents to warm its hollow chambers into life, the landlords of the slums were raising their rents' (John Hollingshead, *Ragged London*, 1861). 'Displaced persons' are not a new twentieth-century pheno-menon: some Westminster parishes were full of them. Old Pye Street, called the most criminal spot of all, is now lined with grim but virtuous buildings, partly the result of that wonderfully generous gift of money made in 1862 for London's poor by George Peabody, the American merchant resident in London who also gave a number of Peabody Museums and other gifts in his own country. Henry Darbishire was architect to the first eight estates built by the Peabody Trust in its first twenty years, and to him is due what has been called their 'intractable external appearance'. But in their stern way these blocks of dwellings gave people roofs and roots and self-respect, and helped to show the way toward public provision of these things.

Some improvements removed the most decayed functions of an old neighbourhood, while leaving livelier functions to renew themselves, a sort of survival of the fittest. Turnmill Street, a raffish little street on the City's north-west border, running along the east bank of the Fleet between Cowcross Street and Clerkenwell Green, was celebrated in Elizabethan plays as a den of disreputable taverns overlooking the foul ditch. The removal of its west side for improvements of the 1850s leading to the construction of the Fleet Sewer and the Metropolitan Railway, while it sent assorted slum-dwellers elsewhere, was doubtless no loss—that side with its flooding cellars and thieves' holes must have been the worst of it. For Turnmill Street cannot entirely have suffered the 'grovelling, starving poverty' Clerkenwell knew in the Forties (*ILN*, 22 May 1847). In directories for 1849 it contained not only four taverns and a common slaughter-man but a whip-thong maker, a smith and bellhanger, and a glass bender, the sort of small expert trades Clerkenwell has long been known for. In 1872 the engravers Grant & Co., of Turnmill Street's remaining east side, published Gustave Doré's *London* (how Doré would have loved the old raffish side of Turnmill Street). From 1901 until 1971, passengers in the Metropolitan Line's open cutting at Farringdon Street Station could look up at the finely sculptured reliefs on a Turnmill Street distillery designed by the architect E. M. Mountford.

The provisioning of London was increasingly performed by railways. Animals still came on the hoof to the live-meat market off Caledonian Road, opened in the early Fifties to relieve the ancient chaos of Smithfield, but the herding of cows and sheep through the streets between certain hours was finally prohibited in 1867. Before that, say at the foot of Ludgate Hill (not yet a 'circus') in 1861, 'at four o'clock in the afternoon, when persons are returning from the City, sheep and cattle from Smithfield, traffic from over the water [via Blackfriars Bridge], and omnibuses from the West-end,—here they all meet'. There were still dairies with resident cows in the centre of town. No. 26 Frith Street has long been what Londoners call a dairy, a small grocer's (not a green-grocer's) shop where milk and other dairy products can be bought. Here, in premises rebuilt about 1735 with a tiny yard behind, the occupier in the 1840s was a

97

H

carver and gilder, succeeded about 1856 by Townsend, cowkeeper, who continued there, presumably with cow. In 1879 Government action was taken, under a recent Contagious Diseases (Animals) Act, to regulate the conditions of cowhouses and dairies. Thereafter 'Townsend, dairyman' appeared in trade directories, presumably without cow, perhaps obtaining his supply from some middleman carting it from an outlying dairy farm. (Soon after 1900 Townsend was succeeded by a dairyman with a Welsh name—the Welsh coming up from the valleys—and another Welsh name has kept the dairy since the Second World War.) Even early in the last century, London's milk supply could not depend on small local one-cow men: there were large 'milk-farms' on the borders of London, with great herds spread across the meadows of Islington, Camden Town, and as we have seen, Battersea Fields, before the railways came and grass gave way to houses. In the late Sixties, milk-cans came to town by railway from as far as 95 miles away (up to 200 miles off when cattle plague affected nearer trade). Some fish came by rail, less quickly and freshly than the fish that still came by boat to Billingsgate but more dependably in bad weather. It is hard to resist Mayhew's descriptions of Billingsgate: 'In the darkness of the shed, the white bellies of the turbots, strung up bow-fashion, shine like mother-of-pearl, while the lobsters, lying upon them, look intensely scarlet from the contrast', and so on.

After a new dead-meat market was built at Smithfield in 1866 (still today, early in the morning, a long brilliantly-lit nave of car-casses), the old Newgate Market off Warwick Lane behind the Prison was closed. Newgate was a half-and-half live- and dead-meat market. Railway vans (some still horse-drawn as late as the 1960s, but no longer) delivered from the nearest railway terminus for Scotland 'long and broad packages, mysteriously shrouded in sack-cloth' in wicker baskets, sides of beef from Aberdeen. Vans seven feet wide containing 'over two tons of meat' crowded into the ten-foot Warwick Lane, where 'the uneven stones, moistened by November fog, afford to the horses' feet about as much easy footing as would a pavement of buttered rolls', to the sound of frantic cursing by their drivers. All this under 'the jaundiced light that gas and daybreak make', where porters ran about, their heads felted with fat, and 'great sides of beef, now unshrouded, hung naked and rosy on giant hooks' while dandy butchers from the West End—whose elegant carts, with 'golden legends on the panels', awaited them outside—decided by mere pokes or pinches and 'paid down their crisp bank-notes and clinking gold' (Greenwood, *Unsentimental Journeys*, 1867). And there was killing on the premises, watched by poor frantic live sheep in dismal dens 'foggy with the steam of blood and departing breath'. After the early hours of wholesaling, 'the leviathans of the market', the big men who despised petty huckstering, closed down and lesser stalls accommodated retail purchasers, poor family men bringing their wives in from Camden Town to buy a week's bony supply at low prices. On Saturday evenings between six and seven more than a thousand persons 'mostly of the better class of mechanics', might be seen issuing from the 'long mazes' of Newgate Market, carrying their next week's meat, end-of-week leavings at reduced prices, as still happens in some butchers' establishments in poorer parts of London today. Further description of London's food supply in 1868 can be found in the *Contemporary Review* for that year. On the site of Newgate Market was eventually built Paternoster Square, to the relief of the publishers of Paternoster Row, nearer St Paul's: 'it is to be hoped that . . . all vestiges of shambles and butchers, with their accompanying nuisances, will have departed to less literary regions' (*Bookseller*, 1870). One of the accompanying nuisances had been the fumes of a tallow-melter living off the market's animal fat in the Row itself. Both Row and Square, with millions of books, were destroyed in the air-raids of December 1940.

The preservation of meat and other foods during long-distance carriage and wholesale storage became a matter of urgent concern in the provisioning of London. It may be indicative that certain firms connected, for example, with pickling, drysaltering and spice-importing were building themselves new premises in the City in the late Sixties, just as in the Seventies a firm that was to play a prominent part in introducing cold-storage shipping of New Zealand and Australian meat was to introduce a new architectural style for its premises in Leadenhall Street (see next chapter). Business was expanding as the population to be fed was expanding.

A prime preserver was vinegar. Messrs Hill, Evans & Co. of Martin's Lane, Cannon Street, made huge vats of it at their Worcestershire factory. When their old London warehouse site was wanted for the Metropolitan and District Railway, they built in 1868 a new depot called Worcester House in Eastcheap (later numbered 33 and 35) with its main front, on this pungent neighbourhood of trade in wine, spices and ginger, done to a spiky design by R. L. Roumieu. Behind this front of red and black brick dressed with

99

stone, moulded brick, tiles and ironwork, it provided offices for the firm and for letting (to various wholesale grocers, solicitors, and so on) on top of two tiers of storage cellars. In other words, it was that desirable combination of spaces that supplanted the old combination of warehouse and counting-house with living quarters. Contemporary stylistic description of the front, 'the Gothic of the south of France with a Venetian impress', need not detain us; it provided office windows sunk in interesting shadow yet large enough to catch what daylight there was in Eastcheap. Even electric light pouring from those Gothic-framed openings into the street mist of a dark winter afternoon is an arresting sight; even with today's teashop inserted, an agreeably sharp-flavoured front. Descriptions of it by today's architectural historians tend to leave out the vinegar.

Another design with the impress of its client's business upon it was William Burges's alteration of a warehouse for Messrs Skilbeck, drysalters of Upper Thames Street, in 1866. This was entirely a warehouse, on the north side of the street. Burges added a new top storey and a new front controlled, in the first place, by the needs of chemical storage: four levels of warehouse doors, two sets of pulleys and a swing crane, and only the few tiny windows suited to a southward exposure for such goods; controlled, secondly, in a design sense, by confining the whole front above the ground floor within the lines of a Gothic two-light arch. If office-size windows had been part of the brief, no doubt Burges would have provided them within that pattern, or another pattern, as for example about the same time, the architect George Aitchison adapted Italian Romanesque round-arched arcades to Nos 59–61 Mark Lane. That was built for renting as counting-houses, or as we say spec-built for offices, for Messrs Innes, wine merchants, not for themselves but as an investment. The arcading, with only single pillars between windows, was a useful formation for buildings on narrow streets, emphasizing openings rather than wall. The narrow streets of Italian cities, with agreeable connotations of princely merchants and exotic foreign trade, were often summoned up by architects of the City of London. But new technologies operated behind the stone or brick screens of street scenery: Aitchison's metal skeleton behind the arcades in Mark Lane; and Burges's iron girder left exposed (but painted) above the ground floor in Upper Thames Street. Burges's colleagues in his profession thought this very bold; perhaps it inspired Scott to leave exposed the girders supporting the corridor bridges lodged in his carriage entry arches at St Pancras. At any rate, the better

City architects, then, thought themselves practical men, even in the ways they clothed their street fronts.

Some architects, indeed, had conservative-minded clients who still preferred plain stuccoed fronts even in the Sixties. Such apparently were Joseph Travers & Sons, wholesale grocers since at least the beginning of the eighteenth century, who built themselves larger premises at what is now No. 119 Cannon Street in about 1866 during the general renovation of that street while the new station and hotel were being finished nearly opposite. Importers of tea, coffee, rice, ginger, and preserved fruits, Messrs Travers also ground and packed spices bought from Dutch importers, and sent the firm's own vessels to Spain for fruit (D. W. Thoms in *Guildhall Miscellany*, April 1970). About a month before Christmas the demand for dried fruit and spices was at seasonal height; by the mid-century more rapid steamships supplanted the schooners dashing under heavy press of canvas across the Bay of Biscay with Christmas fruits to unload at Cox's Wharf near London Bridge (*ILN*, 22 December 1849). The stuccoed plain style of the new building suggests elderly clients and an elderly architect. However thriving and exotic a firm's trade, the funds it might care to spend on its premises could be limited by the plain tastes of its principals. (A descendant of the family was Ben Travers, the celebrated writer of Aldwych farces.)

In May 1866, Lombard Street was the scene of panic when the house of Overend, Gurney at No. 65, at the corner of Birchin Lane a few doors from St Edmund's church, suspended payments. The two compacted rows of commercial houses that formed this vital little street were ranged as closely as any street of palaces in Lombardy. The drama of Black Friday, when anxious crowds rushed to withdraw their money from Barclays and other banks, must have been enhanced by the narrow stage of the street. In the Forties there had been nothing grand or striking there to suggest the 'Californian' treasure within, only a name on a common brass plate at each door (*ILN*, 28 April 1849). But by 1866, the City's biggest building boom since the aftermath of the Great Fire of 1666 had changed much of the scenery. Barclay's, near the east end of the north side, had been rebuilt, faced with bold Tuscan columns, to the design of P. C. Hardwick in 1854–5 (rebuilt since); the London and County (now Westminster) Bank on the south side almost opposite Overend, Gurney had been rebuilt with boldly banded columns in 1861 by Parnell; a little further east, opposite St Edmund's at the corner of Clement's Lane was the newly rebuilt

Royal Insurance Company (1863–4) by J. & J. Belcher, bristling with lion-heads and panels of relief ornament that probably reflected the younger Belcher's studies in France. Royal Insurance Buildings was probably the tallest building in Lombard Street at the time (rebuilt 1910). Our photograph shows that side of the street in 1904 (*Fig. 26*), almost as it had looked in 1866 above the heads of the anxious crowd (but including Waterhouse's Romanesque Clydesdale Bank, built soon after, at the left). Walter Bagehot in 1873 described Lombard Street, symbol of the London money market—that is, the centre of a world network of borrowable money—as 'by far the greatest combination of economical power and economical delicacy that the world has ever seen'. This parade of buildings conveyed the power; the delicacy lay in the web of understandings and arrangements inside. In the early Thirties, William Morris's parents had lived above the premises of the Lombard Street stockbroking firm of which Morris senior was a member. Still in this century caretakers and their families have lived above the empty premises of City firms. A child of the 1920s who grew up on the top storey of Hardwick's Barclays Bank in Lombard Street tells of a fraternity of families visiting across the rooftops and ball-playing in the echoing street after the commuters drained off across London Bridge.

Some sensibilities of the Sixties detested the City building boom. A correspondent signing himself XYZ wrote to the *Builder* in 1863 after a walk through the City that he thought all things old and English and poetic were going: 'there is one prevailing idea—something large, coarse, showy, thick, clumsy, would be grand, but not an idea of any of the tradition of England's sweet poetic loveliness and littleness. . . . We live in an age that hates willow-pattern plates, Dutch tiles, and everything else but show, money, and sin.' (Ten years later that reaction was to take form in Leadenhall Street.) Ruskin railed even more darkly at the architects themselves, at an RIBA meeting in Conduit Street in 1865: cities had become 'mere crowded masses of store, and warehouse, and counter', streets were mere 'drains for the discharge of a tormented mob', every creature was 'only one atom in a drift of human dust and current of interchanging particles, circulating here by tunnels underground, and there by tubes in the air' (perhaps a reference to the tubular railway bridge over the Menai Straits). All this reflected Ruskin's horror of the anarchy of capitalism in 'that great foul city . . . rattling, growling, smoking, stinking,—a ghastly heap of fermenting brickwork, pouring out poison at every pore' (*Crown of Wild Olive*, 1866).

Fig. 26 *Lombard Street, south side, in 1904, as it looked* c. *1870–1910*

Yet poets had long felt horror of London: Wordsworth in his *Prelude* had written aghast at the tides of city life, the 'endless stream of men and moving things', its 'huge fermenting mass of humankind', its 'deafening din'. The city of his youth might in one mood wear 'the beauty of the morning', but it was a 'monstrous ant-hill' too. 'Earth has not anything to show more fair' was not Wordsworth's last word on London. Thus, the nightmare visions of London streets expressed and then partly discarded from Tennyson's *Maud*; so Carlyle on his night walks with Tennyson in the Forties, raving against the 'acrid putrescence' of new buildings in London's chaos.

And William Morris preferred to forget 'six counties overhung with smoke . . . the snorting steam and piston stroke . . . the spreading of the hideous town', and remember an unreal London, 'small, and white, and clean' (*The Earthly Paradise*, 1868). There were other escapes: when in 1855 the pragmatic *Illustrated London News* informed its readers of an increase in insanity in the City, it said that some were 'inclined to attribute this dreadful visitation to excess of eagerness and strife in commercial pursuits . . . and some partially to the effects of railway travelling'. And so through the century there rose and fell waves of feeling about the Metropolis. Meanwhile, the full tide of life at Charing Cross rolled on, surveyed from 1867 by Landseer's bronze lions, guarding Nelson's pedestal at last.

The City of London and Whitehall with Parliament Square were two of the three most influential concentrations of activity in the world in the second half of the nineteenth century. To Whitehall, Scott's sculptural stone palace of Government offices was slowly being added (with quarters for the India Office by M. D. Wyatt), the last part built being the block on Whitehall itself. The third concentration was South Kensington, the great layout intended to realize Prince Albert's ideal precinct of arts and sciences. It was there, in the Sixties, that red brickwork first returned to fashion as a material for major public buildings.

There had indeed been considerable dabbling in red brick during the previous two decades when such brickwork as was left exposed was more usually yellowish or, among conservatives wishing cheaply to emulate stone, white Suffolks. Even in the Thirties, and more in the Forties, the Tudor revival brought back red brickwork, often diapered or chequered with black or blue bricks, for certain sorts of buildings: for schools, hospitals and almshouses (often extensions or replacements of actual Tudor buildings), it was thought to provide 'a sort of homely costume with character'. For commercial buildings, there were experiments in allying red brick with classical styles: as early as 1839 on Bielefeld's papier maché works in Wellington Street, and I'Anson tried it in 1845 on his Royal Exchange Buildings (on the pedestrian way behind the Royal Exchange), a combination of offices, shops and chambers on property said to belong to Magdalen College, Oxford; and there was Sydney Smirke's New Exeter 'Change, a shopping arcade of 'James I' style off the Strand (none of these now exist). About 1857 a law publisher's warehouse in Fetter Lane (derelict in 1971) in the hands of the learned architect Professor Donaldson seemed to reflect his acquaintance with the German work of Schinkel as well as brick buildings of northern Italy. For houses, there was an attempt to introduce a redbrick 'Elizabethan' off New Oxford Street in 1844, but development of that material for private houses had to await further streams of taste: outside London, in the country rectories, cottages and schools by Butterfield and Street and Webb that included the Red House of 1859 by Webb for William Morris; and outside the architectural mainstream, in the partly literary hankering after old Queen Anne mansions expressed by Thackeray in his own Kensington house, No. 2 Palace Green, in 1860, a hankering clearer to him than to us in the still-standing result, realized for him by the architect Frederick Hering. Thackeray's ideas were tempered for Crown approval (since it stands on official property) by supposed imitation—on paper only—of certain details of Wren's Marlborough House, then about to be 'improved' for the Prince of Wales. By 1860 red brickwork began to acquire desirable flavour for a generation conditioned by the creamy shades of well-maintained stucco.

But in some Church of England circles, the warmth of brickwork as a reaction to cool stony classicism was well advanced. A new cult of 'honesty' in church-building in the Forties had reacted especially against the coating of brick with cements and stuccoes. When the silvery grey spire of All Saints, Margaret Street, appeared in the middle Fifties—it is still visible from Oxford Street—and called attention to the black-banded pinkish-red brickwork below, even one non-architectural journal observed that prejudice against brick was quite absurd in a city built, like ancient Babylon, almost entirely of brick. The striation of red brickwork with bands of stone or bricks of other colours, almost with the effect of geological strata, can be traced back to the pages of Ruskin and the influential periodical the *Ecclesiologist*, and to the churches of Butterfield, Street and others. Pearson's modest Lambeth schools' design of 1860, for example (p. 79), called for stock bricks of brownish London clay banded with thin strips of red bricks and Bath stone. During the later Sixties and the Seventies and afterwards, many a cheap secular building or garden wall had its thin red lines among the stocks: the streaky bacon style had set in. Now, we have streaky concrete.

At the mid-century—the pattern of the English nineteenth century, in a sense, placing the early Sixties, or approximately the year of Albert's death, 1861, at 'mid-century'—London's principal public buildings were of stone. These veered in hue from cool (British Museum, Royal Exchange, Public Record Office, Foreign

Office) to warm (Houses of Parliament, Museum of Practical Geology, Buckingham Palace), and all were dirty, encrusted with soot in proportion partly to their age, partly to their openness of exposure to wind and rain, partly to the affinity of certain varieties of stone for acids in the smoky atmosphere. (With the cleaning of stonework going on in London today, since the passage of smoke-control legislation, we now see New Burlington House, for instance, on the north side of Piccadilly as no one has seen it since Charles Barry Jr built it at the end of the 1860s; just as the interior of Westminster Abbey today must be far lighter than for any nine-teenth- or indeed twentieth-century coronation.) With growing interest in warm-hued bricks, there also grew curiosity about impervious materials, tiles, terracottas, marbles, polished granites, glazed bricks, and so on. Ceramic tiles applied to the spire of the Buxton Memorial Fountain now in Victoria Tower Gardens by the river, originally in Parliament Square near Great George Street, still look cheerful. (That is a memorial, by the way, to the abolition of the British slave trade in 1807 and the emancipation of slaves in the British dominions in 1834, and according to its inscription 'was designed and built by Mr Charles Buxton M.P. in 1865, the year of the final extinction of the slave trade and of the abolition of slavery in the United States'. The executant architect was S. S. Teulon. Every one of its eight bronze figures of rulers of England has been stolen, four in 1960 and four in 1971.)

At South Kensington, around 1860, three men especially were involved in buildings for the Royal Horticultural Society (arcades and winter garden, demolished), the South Kensington Museum (north side of present courtyard, Victoria and Albert Museum), and the planning of the International Exhibition (on the present Natural History Museum site). The principal two were Henry Cole, Secretary to the Government Department of Science and Art, who might be called the Genius of South Kensington (or Albert's vicar on earth), and Captain Francis Fowke of the Royal Engineers, who had met Cole at the Paris Exhibition of 1855 and then became super-intendent of buildings at South Kensington. The designer of the sculptural ornament, much of it in terracotta, of the garden and museum buildings, including a cloister of twisted columns in the glass conservatory, was Godfrey Sykes, one of a group of artists associated with Alfred Stevens. There was distinguished interior decoration at the Museum, some of which remains, by Sykes and after his death by Webb and Burne-Jones as members of William

Fig. 27 *International Exhibition under construction at night, early 1862*

Morris's firm. Sykes, incidentally, at Thackeray's request (probably recommended by Cole, who was a friend of the Thackerays), designed the cover of the *Cornhill Magazine* which began publication in 1860. For the Horticultural Society's arcades—long sheltered promenades around the edges of the twenty-two-acre garden—a professional architect, Sydney Smirke, was called in, and he and Fowke deployed styles with all the catholicity of which a museum

107

man (Cole) was capable. Parts of these arcades in purplish-red terracotta remained behind the Imperial Institute till recently.

Fowke was the architect of the Exhibition of 1862, for which work began in the summer of 1861, and the contractors were John Kelk and the Lucas brothers (*Fig. 27*). A permanent gallery for the display of pictures, which had not figured much in Paxton's glass palace, was made part of the complex of exhibition halls: a lofty single-storey affair, 1150 feet in length, with a long series of arcaded windows on Cromwell Road to harmonize with the garden arcades, but made of pale bricks from Sittingbourne in Kent. Parallel with it was a great iron nave joined by domed halls to iron transepts at both ends, and by central vestibules to triple-arched entrances from Cromwell Road and the gardens. In spite of glass roofs and two enormous glass domes, it was not at all a glass palace. The essence of South Kensington public architecture, the modernity of the early Sixties, has been described (by Summerson in an unpublished lecture on the Natural History Museum) as a conglomerate of iron and glass and brick and terracotta. It was neither the modernity of the Coal Exchange nor the modernity of the Crystal Palace; and the next step, in the mid-Sixties, was the conception of the Albert Hall. Meanwhile, owing to an indissoluble muddle of opinions after the Exhibition was over, the removable portions went to make the Alexandra Palace (next chapter) and the 'permanent' picture galleries were blown up: 'succumbing to the irresistible influence of the electric spark applied to the gun-powder with which they were charged, the massive buildings, amidst deathlike silence, suddenly uplifted themselves from the ground, slowly separated in every direction, and finally fell to the earth with thundering crashes' (E. A. Bowring in the *Nineteenth Century*, August 1877).

The Albert Hall (1867–71) was compared by Queen Victoria to the British Constitution, that flexible but solid entity that is such a mystery to foreigners. The Albert Hall is not at all mysterious; it stands on Kensington Gore like an enclosed Colosseum of red brick and terracotta with a glass and iron roof (*Fig. 28*). It was sited on that 'South Kensington axis' created by the symmetry of the Horticultural Society's gardens south of it (the Society departed in the Eighties). On that axis, not only the Albert Hall but the Albert Memorial, the Royal College of Music, the Imperial Institute and the Natural History Museum were 'eventually threaded like onions on a string' (Summerson). The Hall's glowing red exterior, recently cleaned, is crowned by a frieze of figures enacting the arts

Fig. 28 *The opening of the Albert Hall in 1871*

Fig. 29 *The Albert Memorial*

and sciences and a celebratory inscription explaining that the building was erected 'in fulfilment of the intention of Albert Prince Consort', as indeed it was. A concert hall had originally been planned for the 1862 Exhibition, and Fowke's design for the Albert Hall grew from that, and was carried out after his death by another Royal Engineer, H. G. D. Scott; Lucas Brothers were the contractors. The vast interior, like the St Pancras train shed, must be experienced to be believed. It seats thousands in tiers of boxes and upper seats circling an arena of standing or sometimes reclining 'promenaders' (in the summer anyway), and above all is the arcaded gallery with more 'promenaders' as in a painting by Veronese. One project published in 1866 showed the upper level between boxes and gallery (where the steep-set upper seats now are) devoted to the exhibition of a series of large hanging paintings, presumably for a quick look in the interval.

Gilbert Scott's design for a memorial to the Prince Consort was approved in 1863 and finished in 1872, except for the seated figure of Albert (in, as it were, a Madonna's position) by J. H. Foley; that was installed and gilded in 1876 (de-gilded 1915). Scott's design, whatever he said himself, was a splendid elaboration upon an Albert memorial designed by the Manchester architect Thomas Worthington and illustrated in the *Builder* late in 1862. Scott's 'syllabus in stone', as Peter Ferriday calls it (*Architectural Review*, 1964), is an epitome of Victorian sculpture, mosaic and metalwork, a precious reliquary enthroned upon a pyramid of steps (*Fig. 29*). Very fine it looks, especially on a bright day in early autumn against a backdrop of bronzed trees, green grass and blue sky. One thing about it that bothered later generations who singled it out before all Victorian things to jeer at, was the blowing-up of a small-scale art form, a medieval jeweller's shrine, into architecture. Kemp had done it in the Forties in Edinburgh for the Walter Scott memorial, rather topheavily, in a spirit of dour romanticism out of the Gothic north. In Kensington the unrestrained splendour of ornament on Albert's Seat raised the hackles of early-twentieth-century puritans. The cross surmounting it all originally faced north–south on the grand Kensington axis; now the cross faces east–west, as church crosses do. This is not a secular work of art. The contractor, John Kelk, at his own request, built it at no profit to himself and, eventually, in 1874 was made a baronet. Scott, in 1872, was only knighted.

Now for the other end of the axis. The history of the Natural History Museum (for which I am indebted to Summerson's lecture already mentioned) is more complicated, entangled with intentions left over from the 1862 Exhibition. A competition for a separate Natural History branch of the British Museum in 1864 was won by Captain Fowke with a 'mixed North Italian' design rather like the mixture still to be seen on the Victoria and Albert Museum court-yard. Then Fowke died and Alfred Waterhouse was brought in, still under 40 but well known for his Gothic work in Manchester. In the Law Courts competition of 1866–7 he submitted a powerful design which did not win, but parts of it rubbed off on his new Natural History Museum design, which he recast in 1872 (built 1873–80, entirely open by 1886, thus do public works drag on). Questions of style and material were all settled by the spring of 1868. The round-arched twelfth-century style of South Germany, Waterhouse thought, suggested the use of all-over terracotta as such material had been used for Romanesque work in the Rhineland as well as in Lombardy—and the North Italian seam had already been much worked by London architects, high time to try another. Style-choice and material-choice here were made together as for the Coal Exchange: for precision in firing what was a prefabricated covering, pre-cast ornament and all, it was necessary to use only small units, which suited the early style. Some of Fowke's patterns affected Waterhouse's design, but not Fowke's warm red colouring; a buff tone with a little slate-blue inlay was adopted. Incidentally, an obscure architect, Henry Conybeare, who for all we know may have been a friend of Waterhouse, wrote an article in the *Fortnightly* in November 1867 on the future of London architecture, in which he recommended ceramic façades in the style of Romanesque Germany. Waterhouse was a great absorber of suggestions, but that sort of thing was doubtless 'in the air' just then.

The harsh symmetry of the twin-towered entrance and great museum halls must have offended those who growled at 'un-English' grandeur then, as it puts us off today, but it is wonderfully mitigated by the inventive detail of ornament inside, based appropriately on the natural history of animals and fish and plants (*Fig. 30*). There are volumes of drawings in the Museum library showing how Waterhouse created his own ornament in a quite medieval, direct and delightful way for the carver from whose work the terracotta pieces were cast. This was done partly at the suggestion of Professor Sir Richard Owen, the distinguished scientist and director of the Museum, who had sat at the head of the table inside the Iguanodon at Sydenham in 1853. The South Kensington mixture of arts and

Fig. 30 *Natural History Museum, interior detail*

sciences was on the whole well served in the new Museum.

That mixture didn't please everybody, any more than Lombard Street did. For instance a sermon preached to a comfortable suburban congregation on the Queen's Accession Day, 20 June 1869, comparing the reign of Victoria with that of Solomon, observed that godliness was England's security, 'yet how many there are who set up an idol in their hearts. Sometimes it is Gold, sometimes Honour, and sometimes men deify Reason. Perhaps the last is the most dangerous of the three' (sermon preached by the Rev. George Eastman in St Stephen's, Clapham Park). It can, incidentally, be noted that Eastman, the son of a Bethnal Green butcher, had obtained a Cambridge degree after twelve years' study while serving as a curate in Brixton, and had been enabled to finance the building of St Stephen's apparently by the admiring aid of a Brixton spinster, probably the daughter of the type-founder William Thorowgood who, gossips said, seeing Eastman as a curate on the make, forbade her to marry him. At any rate, Eastman was given to writing in a powerful hand letters beginning 'Sir, I have built the above Church', and had cause to despise neither gold nor reason. St Stephen's itself, although built in 1866, was an out-of-date, light-hued Kentish ragstone, Gothic-mixture of a church, with a rural air that had been preferred by comfortable suburban congregations for more than twenty years.

The modern Anglican church of the Sixties was more often made of brick, standing up very tall above the crowded houses of a poor neighbourhood. Such were St Alban's, Brooke Street, Holborn, by Butterfield (1861–2); St Peter's, Kennington Park Road, Vauxhall,

Fig. 31 *St James-the-Less, Westminster, in 1956*

by Pearson (1863–4); two churches at Haggerston, Shoreditch, by James Brooks, St Chad's and St Columba's (1868–9), and many others. Butterfield's All Saints, Margaret Street (pp. 77, 105), and Street's St James-the-Less (p. 38 and *Fig. 31*) were two great forerunners. St Alban's stands in little side streets above Holborn between Gray's Inn Road and Leather Lane street market; the saddleback tower for some years after the last war was a gauntly picturesque semi-ruin, now repaired. Its tremendously tall interior was meant to impress the poor with the warmth of polychromatic construction, mostly yellow and red brickwork in diapers and bands. The church became controversially famous for elaborate ritual, under its vicar Father Mackonochie, but even those who deplored such ritual allowed that it did seem to bring poor people to church for its warmth and light and colour (as gin palaces and music halls did). Some said the poor who came at all only put up with such mysterious goings-on because they were impressed by the real fervour of hard-working priests willing to come and work among the slums. St Peter's, Vauxhall, was the first of a series of structurally interesting London churches by Pearson, vaulted from one end to the other (stone ribs with brick infill), a wonderfully impressive interior not from warmth of colour or ornament but from a sense of cathedral strength. Brooks, too, imparted 'a general air of religiosity' by means of 'dignity and grandeur of proportion [and] solidity of construction' (T. F. Bumpus, *London Churches*). St Chad's until recently was domestically neighboured by the Tudor-style cottages of Nichols Square, above which it stood in its dignity, but taller blocks rise around it now.

And, finally, there were the churches of the very original Samuel S. Teulon, including St Stephen's, Hampstead, of 1869, at the corner of Pond Street and Rosslyn Hill, a vigorous mixture of brickwork and stonework, of French and English Gothic features refracted by Teulon's most individual eye. At the other end of Greater London and of the social scale was his church of St Mark's, Silvertown (*Fig. 32*), beside what is now an elevated highway from Canning Town to North Woolwich, between the Royal Docks and the river. It was set among docks and industry from the first, in 1861–2, after the Victoria Dock (1855) and 'Mr Silver's India-rubber Clothing Works' came to the Essex marshes between the former village of Plaistow and the Thames. Strange in its use of 'structural colour', dark red brick as a sort of protective dado below lighter yellowish brick for the apse, dark above light for a turret like a

Fig. 32 *St Mark, Silvertown, in 1944*

smoke-stack, St Mark's has an upthrust pyramid of a spire buttressed by the upthrust cone of the apse: not so much a beacon to sailors, as other riverside churches were, but a beacon across old marshes heavy with new cranes and new drainage works, sour with new industrial smells. It serves the dockers' community of little old houses and new heights of flats that look down on giant hulls and funnels.

There was a dauntlessness and sweep about many of the building schemes of the Sixties, an inability to be trivial. On another plane, there was the often unsuitable vastness of women's crinolines, which reached their greatest circumference about 1860 and toward 1865 swelled even more at the rear. This 'distended drapery' was a thoroughly 'obnoxious obstruction', said some men who lived with it, in theatres, omnibuses, trains, dining rooms, on the stairs, and in many a situation in private life; *Punch* in 1861 had a Hints-to-Architects drawing showing the lower half of a church doorway extra-chamfered for wide skirts. Book illustration in the Sixties attained a monumentality it did not in that century attain again; this included, especially, periodicals such as the *Cornhill*, where for example George Du Maurier's illustrations for Mrs Gaskell's *Wives and Daughters* appeared from August 1864 until January 1866. The uncluttered sweep of lines and forms in the best of these wood-engravings seems to have something to do with a large flow of skirts and with solid pieces of uncluttered furniture, as well as with the direct largeness of the artist's vision of contemporary people in the small pages of this black-and-white art.

There was monumental uneasiness, too, at the end of the Sixties which we in our day ought to be able to appreciate. Some of the worries of the time—about standing armies on the Continent, or about the effects of greater democracy granted in the new Reform Act, or about man's place in the universe—affected the fabric of London only indirectly. But there was a deep worry felt only by a few, comparable to the one about pollution in our day before that became fashionable.

An editorial leader in the *Clapham Gazette* for October 1870 ruminated on the German siege of Paris and on the human race, in general and in England: 'the boasted civilisation about which the comfortable classes are ever ready to speak as the climax of human progress, is only a film or screen to conceal the most ferocious and savage instincts.' That was probably Meaden, who chaired local Board of Works meetings and knew how the *un*comfortable classes lived. The editor of the *Builder*—George Godwin, architect and author of *Town Swamps and Social Bridges* (1859) and other outspoken books—put it equally forcibly: 'If the lessons of the past decade do not induce us to set our own house in order, our children may have to write—*Anglia fuit*.' It was not City panic or Hyde Park riot that men like Godwin and Meaden meant, but conditions of bricks and mortar, familiar as they were with the annual reports of London's district medical officers, every one driving home the connection between savage living conditions and savage infant mortality or warping for life. Central urban improvements that crowded out the poorest drove the 'removed poor' to settle in any corner they could, even as far as Fulham, where later in the century Charles Booth noted the history of its south-eastern corner as 'a dumping ground for London' with all the signs of a new criminal quarter. When in 1865 the Medical Officer of Health for Fulham (quoted by Jephson) reported the terrible overcrowding in his district resulting from 'tremendous demolition' of houses in central London and lack of provision for the increase in the outward 'human tide', that sober official burst out that it 'certainly could not have been intended by Providence' that of all the children born, nearly one-half should die before the age of five. Today's echo is the voice of a Minister of Transport (*The Times*, 7 July 1971): 'There is no unalterable law which requires that half the children born today will at some time be injured in a road accident.' We shape our cities and afterwards our cities shape us.

Fig. 33 Downstream: London Bridge in 1872

Fig. 34 Upstream: Albert Bridge

CHAPTER FIVE

The Seventies: Art and the Money Fabric

The channelling of London's tidal forces and the founding of large institutions of arts and sciences gave a stern purposeful tone to the period just summarized. Yet beside all those people making purposeful impressions upon London, it would be unfair to forget the artists who set down the impressions London made on them. There had been anecdote-tellers like Frith who, after spending more than a year painting his long canvas of the crowds in Paddington Station, said he saw nothing picturesque in Paddington Station itself. (Think what Monet saw in the Gare St Lazare; if only Monet had painted the steamy interior of St Pancras's vast shed.) There were romantic recorders of London night scenes like Henry Pether and Atkinson Grimshaw. Pether's view of Trafalgar Square, in the London Museum, faithfully recorded what could be seen by moonlight there, just before Landseer's lions were added, with the Percy lion still aloft on Northumberland House; Grimshaw's views from bridges along the river had a more haunting poetry in them. There was no one quite like the great poet Turner, born so near the urban Thames that his vision first was formed by shifting vaporous light along the King's Reach between Westminster and London Bridge.

Whistler had arrived in 1859 and found out the fascination of the river, at first in the busy life of barges and ships below London Bridge; the Thames was much busier then than now, the upstream traffic thickening on a rising tide, with collapsible masts on the smaller shipping above bridge. His 'Thames set' of etchings made in the Sixties at Wapping and Rotherhithe vibrate with 'wonderful tangles of rigging, yardarms and rope; farragos of fog, furnaces and corkscrews of smoke; the profound and intricate poetry of a vast capital', as Baudelaire put it when these etchings reached Paris (quoted by Denys Sutton in Colnaghi catalogue, 1971). In 1863 Whistler had moved to a house overlooking the quieter reach of river at Chelsea, where the water glimmered mysteriously away toward the shores of Battersea, rimmed by modest warehouses and wharves between old Battersea Church and new Battersea Park. In several paintings he immortalized the old wooden bridge, poeticizing it into something out of a Japanese print; the one in the Tate Gallery was first shown at the Grosvenor Gallery when that was opened in the spring of 1877. In his 'nocturnes' of the Seventies, patterns of real ships, buildings, and bridges began to dissolve in atmospheres or, rather, moods of the river in brown and silver or blue and gold —a poetry of river-moods where his earlier Thames scenes had a poetry of river-patterns.

In 1870 several young French painters escaped the German invasion of France by coming to London: Daubigny, Monet, Pissarro. Paul Durand-Ruel, the Paris dealer with faith in this young generation, had already set up a London branch at 168 New Bond Street, a two-storey building now incorporated in Asprey's shop (the Peacock Room was to be shown at No. 168 in 1904). Durand-Ruel paid Pissarro 200 francs and Monet 300 francs apiece for each picture he took and did his best to sell them, unsuccessfully, to a world that now sits in Sotheby's up the road, watching them knocked down for huge ransoms. Pissarro, lodging in Norwood, painted suburban roads with the Crystal Palace in the background. Monet painted the Thames, one view of 1871 (now a legacy from Lord Astor to the National Gallery) showing a pattern of embankment construction and steamboats against a misty Westminster Bridge and Houses of Parliament with a fantastically elongated Clock Tower. French artists seemed to have been brought up on fairy tale giant-pinnacled fantasies such as Doré placed on the horizon beckoning Dick Whittington—half Perrault fairy story, half St Pancras.

Pieces of seventeenth-century London still stood about, for all the improvements and demolitions, the threading with pipes and rails, the expensive new columns and extra storeys. Young architects looking for a different set of old ideas to revive in 1870 had only to walk about Holborn, the City, and Westminster to find them. There were still two-storey bay windows flanked by giant pilasters at Nos 184–5 Fleet Street (demolished 1892) and at No. 413 Strand with little pediments and over all an elaborate cornice. Below such

Fig. 35   *New Zealand Chambers, Leadenhall Street, about 1900*

windows there might be dado panels, curved or flat, carved in ornate relief: the front of Sir Paul Pindar's house in Bishopsgate, removed for an extension of Liverpool Street Station in 1890 and now in the Victoria and Albert Museum, has them. There had been arched glazing bars for such windows in Great Winchester Street earlier in the century and doubtless some were still around, there were small-paned Georgian shopfronts here and there which no one had bothered to modernize, there were oval windows in Wren churches. Steep-sided broken pediments still decorated chimney-pieces in old taverns. In short, all the paraphernalia of the gay façade put together in 1871–2 by Richard Norman Shaw to surprise the merchants of the City and the Royal Academy (*Fig. 35*).

A good many words have been said about that front, as a new smile on the face of ancient Leadenhall Street, but behind it on the deep site New Zealand Chambers consisted of a very practical series of blocks linked by a spinal corridor. When John Tallis printed his view of Leadenhall Street in 1838, Nos 34 and 35 on the south side west of Billiter Street were four-storeyed, rebuilt or refronted in the eighteenth century with small-paned shopfronts, and No. 35's two main storeys over the shop were flanked by a pair of giant pilasters. The Edinburgh & London Steam Shipping Co. occupied No. 35; in 1838 there was only one other shipping firm in the street. By 1870, the street was full of ship brokers: British shipping, between one half and one third of the world's total tonnage, was the visible instrument of British economic power in the world. No. 34 in 1838 was occupied by an oil-and-colour merchant; in 1870 the oil merchant was still there, probably on the ground floor, and the other occupiers were Shaw Savill & Co., ship brokers. In 1858, two young men working for one of the shipping firms serving the growing emigrant traffic to New Zealand, Robert Ewart Shaw and Walter Savill, had left to found their own firm, in Billiter Street at first. By 1866, Shaw Savill were chartering and despatching sixty-eight ships a year, and by then they owned some of the speediest sailing vessels afloat. By the end of the Seventies, refrigeration of meat cargoes from Australia and North America became practicable, and in 1882 Shaw Savill combined with the rival Albion Line to build and run their own line of steamers. By 1868, Shaw's architect brother had been designing a country house, Leys Wood in Sussex, for Temple, another member of the firm.

New Zealand Chambers, on the site of the old Nos 34 and 35, was built not only for Shaw Savill's own offices but for letting: by 1880 it contained twenty-seven firms, many of them shipping agents. Needless to say, only a few had the glamorous new windows of the Leadenhall Street front (the lining of the areas between the rear blocks with white glazed tiles was not entirely new, but already a City practice in the Sixties—like the oblique reflecting panels outside so many City windows, hoarding light in narrow lanes and light-wells as cisterns in desert countries hoard water). The éclat of the new front on Leadenhall Street, with its red brick and white trim, can only be imagined now, New Zealand Chambers having been bombed in the war and the whole scale of the street having changed since. The two buildings flanking it in our old photograph were lower affairs when Shaw's building first appeared. But what a change from the ponderous new buildings of the Sixties in Lombard Street, or the grandeur of the new National Provincial Bank in Bishopsgate (1865, by John Gibson, carrying on the palatial single-storey tradition of Soane's Bank of England). However, Shaw's piquant and practical building is not quite so surprising when we remember the Eastcheap vinegar depot, no matter how different their 'styles'. Street architecture now had either a *palazzo* character or a piquant-and-practical character.

To older architects, Shaw's new (miscalled) 'Queen Anne' Revival raked up 'a type of the very lowest state of corrupt erections, of a

123

period that marks the senility of decaying taste', and seemed 'like the last somersault or gambol of the agile gymnast who seeks to extort a laugh at the end of his performance': so Professor Donaldson, at almost eighty. Yet Donaldson's own 'Tudor' front of 1848 on the west side of Gordon Square (former University Hall) separates banks of windows with tall narrow piers, and in 1853 he was recommending the 'lost picturesqueness' of old curved brick gables in Kent as a welcome change from the 'insipidity' of hipped roofs; in a sense, the situation in 1873 was 'where he came in'.

A whole community exemplifying the Queen Anne Revival was shortly to arise, full of the lost picturesqueness of brick gables and the opposite of insipid to this day (*Fig. 36*). In the first place, there was a wholesale woollen warehouse in Warwick Street, Golden Square, Westminster. Apparently started in the Thirties by three Carrs from Cumberland, the firm was Carr & Son in the early Seventies and had expanded its premises by 1875. In that year, Jonathan T. Carr, aged all of 30, was enabled one way or another to buy forty-five acres of land near the recently opened Turnham Green station on the new railway line between Richmond and the City, on which to lay out an estate with a difference. Bedford Park, as it was to be called, was to be for people with artistic inclinations. Possibly the woollen business had dealings with Morris & Co. in Queen Square? Or did the temporary proximity of William Morris himself—at a house on Turnham Green between 1872 and 1878—influence Carr at all? Carr had been one of ten children, not the eldest, in a not apparently 'aesthetic' family, although he and his younger brother J. Comyns Carr (who helped to found the Grosvenor Gallery) found their own ways into aesthetic circles. Eastlake's *Hints on Household Taste* and the first part of Morris's *Earthly Paradise* had both come out in 1868 when Jonathan Carr was 23; in a sense, his ideal for Bedford Park seemed a fusion of the two. He had as well, as we shall see (next chapter), an incurable itch for speculation. At any rate, in 1876 Carr commissioned E. W. Godwin and then, in 1877, Norman Shaw and eventually other architects to design prototype houses for the estate (as more fully told by T. A. Greeves in *Country Life*, December 1967), and Shaw also designed the church, the inn, and 'the stores'. The resulting colony of detached and semi-detached red-brick houses, with small-paned windows, white-painted glazing bars and balconies, and rubbed-brick details of seventeenth-century sorts, was not only quaint but most of the three-storey non-basement houses were well planned.

Fig. 36 *Bedford Park*

Carr had sensed among his contemporaries a growing demand for middle-sized sensible houses for middle-class young couples whose household tastes did not run to the more vertical villas of Fulham or Gospel Oak, and whose incomes could not manage Kensington or Brompton. That generation in the Seventies, especially among young professional men, journalists, writers and artists with uncertain incomes and expanding social and cultural tastes, was beginning to limit the number of its children: birth control as a social trend is about a century old. As for their household tastes, not all of them cultivated the Bedford Park brand of Morris-wallpaper simplicity. Some liked to see, for example, elaborate gilt-framed flower paintings on the door-panels of their drawing rooms or dining rooms. Almost everybody liked a bit of stained glass, around the front door and on the staircase, a usage that came out of the Gothic Revival and provided uncurtained privacy with jewel-like colour. The urge for more colour could also express itself in Mr Liberty's fabrics.

Around the time of the 1862 Exhibition, Arthur Lasenby Liberty, aged barely 20, had been taken on as manager by Farmer & Rogers's Oriental warehouse, a depot for goods from the Far East at 171–5 Regent Street. The firm was then selling some of the Japanese exhibits from the Exhibition. This trend in its trade seems to have grown out of the firm's dealings in shawls, those important Early and Mid-Victorian articles of dress. About 1861, Farmer & Rogers advertised themselves as 'the great shawl and cloak emporium . . . India, China, French, Paisley, Norwich, and Fancy Shawls'; earlier predecessors in their premises in the giant-pilastered block of Nash's Regent Street (west side just above New Burlington Street) at the beginning of Victoria's reign had been a firm of 'Shawl Dealers'. In the Sixties Farmer & Rogers also imported Oriental wares such as porcelain, lacquer-work, screens, and colour prints, as well as embroideries and other fabrics, all of which soon fascinated people like Whistler, who had visited a similar shop in Paris, and Rossetti and others. (Yet there had been a Japanese Exhibition in London as early as 1854, when 'a singular cargo of curiosities' was placed on public view in Pall Mall East, furniture, bronzes, porcelain, silks, and paintings, 'very curious' and likely to be 'very attractive' according to the *Illustrated London News* in February, but apparently then the attraction did not 'take'.)

In 1875 Liberty started his own shop on the other side of Regent Street, three doors below the entry to Great Marlborough Street, on part of the present site of Liberty & Co. Here he not only met the growing demand for Oriental fabrics but stimulated English silk and woollen manufacturers, makers of dyes, and designers such as Godwin. Behind Liberty's influence on orientalizing taste and Morris's influence on medievalizing taste, their parallel stimulus toward higher standards of design and quality of materials worked on the fabric trades.

The year 1875 also saw the designing by Norman Shaw of an 'artistic business elevation in creamy coloured woodwork' for a new shop in Oxford Street, on the west corner of Chapel Street, for Murray Marks, a young dealer in precious wares including Oriental porcelain. Shop windows having been for a generation opened up by great sheets of glass as much as was then possible, the reaction here was to divide the shop window into a few small niches for precious objects, one *sang-de-bœuf* pot set off by a blue-and-white piece here and a glowing bit of lacquer there. Marks's trade card device of peacock feathers and a ginger jar was said to have been designed by Rossetti, Whistler and Morris jointly. The London cult for blue-and-white porcelain in the Seventies and Eighties was assiduously and discriminatingly fostered by Marks. He also acted as general adviser to that patron of the arts Frederick Richard Leyland, founder of a line of steamers from Liverpool and 'the last man in Liverpool who wore frills habitually'—certainly not as an elderly survival from the Regency might cling to his shirt frills, for Leyland at the beginning of the Seventies was only 40. He had presumably made much of his wealth by then, and about this time there was in London a group of moneyed and/or artistic young men who affected knee breeches and buckled shoes, some years before Oscar Wilde added to that aesthetic costume a lily in his medieval hand.

People said that Leyland dreamed of living the life of an old Venetian shipping merchant in modern London. His way of going about it was to take a negative but capacious exterior, one of the large dull houses in Prince's Gate, Exhibition Road, and transform the interior. He had the aid of Norman Shaw, recommended by Marks. Shaw divided the drawing rooms by a pair of semi-Gothic screens, made of carved walnut panels and brass openwork, often said to have been inspired by a Flemish rood-screen that had recently reached the South Kensington Museum through the hands of Murray Marks but really quite unlike it—so much have the legends about this house become blurred. On some of the ceilings neo-Jacobean pendants dripped gas lamps. As a collector of paintings, Leyland leaned towards Rossetti, Burne-Jones, and Botticelli: Rossetti's *Blessed Damozel* was his, and Burne-Jones's *Circe*, and Botticelli's four Decameron panels from the Pucci collection. A taste for Italian painters before Raphael was developing in just those few collectors who already had a taste for the English Pre-Raphaelites. In the year the Botticellis were bought, 1874, when all this house decoration was under way, Leyland acquired the marble staircase from Northumberland House in Trafalgar Square, presumably split for use at Prince's Gate; it was not a Jacobean or even eighteenth-century piece, but was ascribed to the architect Thomas Cundy (died 1825), and the ormolu balustrade consisted of great leafy scrolls, perhaps modelled on a pre-Nash staircase at Buckingham Palace. (Another Leyland house, belonging to Thomas Naylor Leyland, in Knightsbridge, demolished 1961 when it was the Royal Thames Yacht Club, contained a very similar staircase, perhaps by one of the Cundys, but that would be coincidence.) For the wall of the Prince's Gate staircase Whistler designed dado panels imitating Japanese lacquer designs, just the sort of thing middle-income house-owners then proceeded to imitate.

Murray Marks also recommended a decorator for the dining room that was to contain Leyland's collection of blue-and-white porcelain: Thomas Jeckyll. The oldest person involved here though not yet 50, Jeckyll was both architect and designer (perhaps best summed up by Peter Ferriday in the *Architectural Review* for August 1959). His most recent London work then included a billiard room designed for Alexander Ionides in Holland Park Road, its walls and ceiling a deft arrangement of panels in a Japanese-like wooden framework grid, which for Leyland's jugs and bowls in 1876 he translated three-dimensionally into an arrangement of shelves and cages. Behind and below these he covered the walls with panels of Cordovan leather with small red patterns on it. Jeckyll had perhaps heard of a vogue for leather wall-coverings in the Forties, when the *Illustrated London News* reported the lining of several rooms at Chatsworth 'with the new painted leather, superbly relieved in different colours, intermixed with a profusion of gold' (*ILN*, 21 May 1842). Leyland's was said to be old leather brought to England by Catherine of Aragon, a valuable object of art in itself and a quietly sumptuous background for the porcelain. How Whistler swept in to bring the room into harmony with his own picture bought to hang over the fireplace, gradually painting over the leather as if it were canvas, has been many times told. His new scheme of peacocks and their feathers covered the entire room including the window shutters with turquoise and gold. Leyland accepted the accomplished fact, and Jeckyll in late 1876 went out of his mind and so remained until his death in 1881. The room was dismantled after Leyland's death in 1892 and went eventually, via Detroit, to the Freer Gallery in Washington. The house remained a treasure-house only during Leyland's lifetime. The treasure dispersed in 1892 and originally amassed from steamship lines out of Liverpool was one of the major collections in any account of London art collectors of the nine-teenth century, and points also to the outdistancing of London shipping by Liverpool in the last quarter of the century.

Art collecting was not all on the scale of Leyland or Ionides or Holford, nor were works of art always inherited on the lordly scale of the Dukes of Westminster and Sutherland or the Earl of Elles-mere. Even in the Forties, Waagen the German historian of English collections observed that 'whosoever would wish to see the rich resources of this country in works of art, must pierce into private houses—into back parlours and attics, as well as drawing-rooms' (quoted in *ILN*, 23 June 1849). One shrewd observer of the Seventies, T. H. S. Escott, noticed that an interest in art was by then a great leveller, an instrument of a new kind of class fusion; the professional house decorator was no longer a mere tradesman, the architect and artist were socially not only acceptable but interesting. It might be quite illuminating to analyse the origins of all the early residents of Bedford Park, that community of the artistically-inclined founded by the woollen-merchant's son, even though little art was actually produced there (as time went on, some people felt that their way of life there was rather a work of art). Some practising artists lived well in, say, Melbury Road, Kensington (Marcus Stone at No. 8, Luke Fildes at No. 11, both houses by Norman Shaw), or around the corner in Holland Park Road (Leighton's house by George Aitchison), or in Fitzjohn's Avenue, Hampstead (Frank Holl at No. 6, Edwin Long at No. 61, again both by Shaw). Prosperous lawyers, as always, lived well but not all of them in such modern style as Wickham Flower, for whom Shaw in 1875 designed Swan House on Chelsea Embankment, a house deco-rated by Morris & Co.: even though Morris himself disliked the 'debased-classical' features of the Queen Anne Revival, the clients of architects such as Shaw liked Morris's papers and fabrics. These areas attracted more houses in the Shaw manner, the *avant garde* fashion of the Seventies. Not everyone had houses like that.

In the vicinity of Brixton, Camberwell, Finsbury Park, and Upper Holloway, people inhabited 'frail tenements of clay and fir' bearing 'a Cockneyfied stamp of Gothicesque or Italianesque', houses of moderate size manufactured 'to supply an unceasing demand': that was *Building News* in 1874 complaining of the 'reckless amount of scamped work in the suburbs of London'. Rising artisans, or City clerks like Mr Pooter in the Nineties, lived in those. Only toward the end of the century did the balustraded balconies and 'Dutch' gables of Bedford Park filter down to new houses of that sort. But responsible efforts were being made to achieve more solid houses for working men's families. On the old market garden ground of Battersea Fields was rising Shaftesbury Park, one of the chief estates created by an Artizans', Labourers' and General Dwellings Company (its history has been given by J. N. Tarn in *Architectural Review*, May 1968). Shaftesbury Park's streets of two-storey houses in solid terraces of yellow brick are still in good repair.

Above the sea of roofs in these suburbs there began to rise the new primary schools, authorized under the Education Act of 1870 and built by the newly created London School Board (*Fig. 37*). The architect to the Board, E. R. Robson, described what he and the other architects concerned were doing in a book published in 1874, though only in the second edition of 1877 did he feel it necessary to explain the style of the new schools, then and now regarded as pioneer examples of the so-called Queen Anne Revival, taking this as a suitable London-brick, seventeenth-century vernacular. Although some of the outside architects who designed for the Board at first used red brickwork, Robson felt that the yellowish London stocks (varying through brownish shades when dirty) were more impervious to London weather; schools designed by him generally used these dressed with stone and softer red brick. Later erosion of such trimmings brought about the use of harder and less appealing materials. The memorable thing about these schools is their height, often enclosing a play area on the ground floor, and the picturesque variety of roofs and gables.

If one new London building type sought its background in local tradition, another—that of the new restaurants—borrowed a sort of international 'fancy style' partly from Paris, partly from indigenous theatres and music halls. One of the best of these was Thomas Verity's Criterion Restaurant. In spite of alterations and electric signs its front on the south side of Piccadilly Circus is still (developers permitting) one of the few of its type left. Restaurants are to

Fig. 37 *Board School, Caledonian Road, after a drawing by H. W. Brewer*

be part of the next chapter on the Eighties, when they became even more numerous, but as a social note on the Seventies it should be mentioned that Simpson's Dining Rooms in the Strand, the St James's Restaurant in Piccadilly, and the Burlington Restaurant in Regent's Street among others all had ladies' dining rooms (Baedeker, 1879). The Café Royal's Domino Room, now surviving in part as its grill room, seems to date from the early Seventies: a famous interior recorded by so many artists in words and paint, with its gilt, its wreathed caryatids, its mirrors like mirrored window-shutters

131

reflecting so many famous faces. The architects, Archer & Green, then proceeded to build Cambridge Terrace, a strangely Victorian presence in Regent's Park, and one wonders if their anonymous client came from the restaurant world.

Money shepherded by lawyers and bankers continued to fertilize London property. It would be crudely simplifying to say that New Zealand Chambers was the product of money made from outward-bound passenger cargoes plus home-bound meat cargoes; that Bedford Park was possibly a product of money made in a woollens' warehouse in a back street off Regent Street; that Melbury Road, Kensington, was the product of money inherited or made by clients of the artists who lived there; that the new Board Schools were only the product of money inherited or made by the taxpayers. Not to mention the borrowed money financing most London property ventures: 'English trade is carried on upon borrowed capital to an extent of which few foreigners have an idea' (Bagehot, *Lombard Street*, 1873). The built fabric of any city is an outward and visible sign of its pecuniary fabric, as much as it is of the fabric of architects' dreams and drawings. Architects' dreams barked their shins on pecuniary fabrics then as now. The fact that architecture was an art, as well as the product of the devices and desires of clients' hearts, was sometimes hard to detect in the Seventies when many buildings were of the fussy quality of the Horseshoe Hotel, Tottenham Court Road. In general, except for splendid gas lamps and cut-glass panels, the sheer effrontery of gin palaces compared to that of commercial buildings was less than in the Thirties.

Much of London was built on honest or at any rate sanguine speculation. But, in the Seventies especially, swindlers rose to meet a get-rich-quick philosophy like the railway mania of the Forties. There is evidence that some of the idle ground on Victoria Street was tilled by one or two of these. Oddly enough, from one outstanding specimen, London profited. Leicester Square garden, where marble Shakespeare broods above the benches and pigeons, is the only visible mark left on London by one of the best-known public men of the Seventies. Which is just as well. The vicissitudes of this private ground, during the lifetime of most people then living, had been those of some modern bombed site: hoardings, weeds, rubbish, vandals, temporary buildings, legal tangles among a group of owners. Over the years *Punch* had isolated a new species of nettle, 'a real Leicestersquariensis, four feet high', and George I's statue was reduced to a sick joke (*Fig. 38*). In January 1874, just as the Metro-

Fig. 38 *Leicester Square about 1870, a rare view showing George I's horse still in place*

politan Board of Works was finally in a position to acquire the garden at last for the public, a certain Baron Grant told them that he was about to do so, having been 'for some months past . . . in negotiation . . . for the purchase of the ground with a view to laying it out as a garden, and handing it over to the Board as a gift to the Metropolis'.

Albert Grant, born Gottheimer in Dublin in 1830, emerged on the London public scene in 1865 as M.P. for Kidderminster and managing director of the so-called Credit Foncier & Mobilier of England with offices at 17–18 Cornhill (previously the lavish premises of Sarl & Sons, silversmiths). Some years earlier, an Albert Gottheimer was partner in a firm of wine importers in Mark Lane: the basis, perhaps, of the story that he was 'educated in London and Paris'. In 1865 he is said to have put up a great deal of the money for the building of the Galleria Vittorio Emmanuele in Milan, that is, he floated the City of Milan Improvements Company Ltd, the client for this great cruciform arcade, the building of which was largely a British enterprise. Grant's reward was a title conferred by

133

King Victor Emmanuel II in 1868; at that time it must have meant much to Piedmontese pride to confer kudos in the name of Italy. Grant's barony was no emptier than many an English one—whatever the wits said later of a 'barren grant'—and the Galleria still flourishes, a splendidly parvenu scene for urban life. So far, so good. Now Grant was a pioneer of mammoth company promoting in England, blandly issuing prospectuses for Lima Railways, Lisbon Tramways, Odessa Waterworks, the Imperial Bank of China and the Emma Silver Mine in an international network of speculation of which he was only a part. The Baron's particular bit of finesse was to concentrate on lists of small investors, clergymen and widows who were only too anxious to invest: he gambled on the gambling spirit of little people. The character of the giant speculator Augustus Melmotte, M.P., in Trollope's novel *The Way We Live Now* was created in Trollope's study in Montagu Square in 1873 while Grant was still riding high, yet Melmotte's downfall was a macabre prediction of Grant's downfall that was to become obvious only in 1876. He was at his zenith in 1874, when he rescued Leicester Square, bought the *Echo* newspaper, and was re-elected to Parliament. The grand gesture of giving the Square garden to the public of London smacks of a private hope that, if Victor Emmanuel gave a barony for the Galleria, surely Victoria might offer some English honour. Grant's gesture, often called the redeeming feature of a flamboyant career, wasn't meant to be made for nothing; he made a similar offer later in the year to improve Soho Square (not accepted), just to underscore the point.

The Leicester Square garden was laid out for Grant by James Knowles, by then editor of the *Contemporary Review* and a friend of Tennyson, and designer of a great parvenu house for Grant in Kensington. The statue of Shakespeare was adapted from the eighteenth-century monument in Westminster Abbey, but with an inscription from *Twelfth Night*: 'There is no darkness but ignorance.' Was there no lapidary tongue-in-cheek on someone's part, in so recalling the clown's assurance to Malvolio? At any rate, it was in a sense Grant's shareholders, 'more puzzled than the Egyptians in their fog', who involuntarily gave the Leicester Square garden to the public of London. Long before *It's a long way to Tipperary, farewell Leicester Square* became the hit song of the First World War, the Bard was on his pedestal presiding over the marble basin fed by dolphins spurting water from their heads, like cherub-whales spouting. Four busts of eminent neighbourhood residents, on bases like up-ended soap-boxes, stand awkwardly isolated in the corners of the garden.

Within a year or so after the dedication ceremony in 1874, the baseless fabric of the mammoth promoter's vision and all his cloud-capped companies began to dissolve. By 1877 eighty-nine legal actions against him were pending. In the spring of that year Grant's collection of pictures, mostly bought *en bloc* to furnish the new house, were sold off at Christie's. His last public-spirited gesture had been to lend one of them, a Maclise, to the Royal Academy in 1875. Its subject was Shakespearian, *The disenchantment of Bottom*, with a long quotation from Bottom in the catalogue: 'I have had a dream, past the wit of man to say what dream it was: man is but an ass, if he go about to expound this dream. . . .'

At least we can smile at Baron Grant and thank him for Leicester Square. The Seventies in the (once more) United States were much worse. The spiritual aftermath of a bitter war, described so well as 'brown decades' by Lewis Mumford, clothed buildings in funereal brownstone and iron. In England, where there had been no war, the constructions and cotton famine of the Sixties left casualties, and the human waste of poverty went on. But London's most modish new buildings were clothed in cheerful red brick and terracotta.

On the same day of July 1874 that Leicester Square was ceremoniously opened, the Percy lion was being removed from Northumberland House a few hundred yards away. He found a new pad at Syon House, but his old palace and its garden were doomed to be replaced by a new avenue linking Trafalgar Square to the new Victoria Embankment. Ironically enough, just as modish new architects were playing with neo-Jacobean ideas on their drawing-boards (as in the very house in Prince's Gate to which the old staircase went), the grand Jacobean frontispiece on Trafalgar Square's south-east side was auctioned off for the price its materials could fetch as second-hand bricks and building stone. This destruction was said at the time to be 'much regretted by many men of taste' as a 'needless act of Vandalism', since it was felt that the avenue could have begun just south-west of Northumberland House, merely slicing off part of the garden (Walford, *Old and New London*, *c.* 1878). Augustus Hare thought the house would make an admirable National Portrait Gallery. Nor had the family treasures inside been entirely barred to public gaze, to excuse the ignorance insisting upon this removal. During the summer of the Great Exhibition of 1851, for example, this unique house ranged about its courtyard had been thrown open to the public and thousands trooped through its great rooms decorated in the eighteenth century. The gardens behind had been neglected, not surprisingly; even before the long building-mess of road, underground railway, and sewer works along the Embankment, the gardens were too near the smells of the river. So that strange wilderness near the busy Strand, when at last the garden walls came down, 'was somewhat sad and ghastly, the old hawthorns and hazels looking like Dryads of old suddenly exposed to the gaze of an irreverent troop of Satyrs', the demolition men. The erection of Charing Cross Railway Station almost next door had been the beginning of the end.

Northumberland Avenue, a counterfeit of Paris but a tired-looking one, with its long tall fronts so boringly decorated and its north-west–south-east orientation that seems in this latitude to exclude the sun more often than not, has never been one of the delights of London. The only thing to be said for it, it is shorter than Victoria Street. Contemporary comment was outspoken after its most prominent site, the rounded corner with Trafalgar Square and the Strand, was weighed down by the seven-storey Grand Hotel of 1878 (by Messrs Francis): 'the most vulgar corner in London', 'the new Charing Cross style . . . representing money without culture', and so on. And indeed, if the time comes to demolish this ponderously curved and honeycombed mass of littleness—quite like the elder Brueghel's painting of *The Tower of Babel* at Rotterdam—not a hand should be lifted, and all energy and discrimination devoted to getting a better successor on such a site. Not, as was predicted in 1873 when the impending sale of Northumberland House was announced, 'building in its place some staring vulgar monstrosities'. But there are other possibilities (pp. 152–3).

The Grand Hotel (now Grand Buildings) and its neighbours were not alone in failing to meet the new challenge to building design afforded by improved mechanisms, of lifts for people and hoists for building materials. How high should one go by placing one brick upon another? As high as Queen Anne's Mansions, was one answer. The tallest portions of London's first skyscraper (demolished 1971) were of fourteen storeys, with a wall thickness near to four feet at its base. The name referred to no ornamental revival whatever, but to its position near Queen Anne's Gate, Westminster, on a prominent site at the corner of Broadway and Petty France, looming above the Guards' Chapel and Birdcage Walk and over-bearing the landscape of St James's Park, a dreadful precedent for present-day invasions of other park horizons in London. Its spiritual home was Victoria Street nearby. An entirely unprofessional speculator, Henry A. Hankey, seems to have started this block of flats to his own design, if this hulk of bricks could be said to have one in 1875. The Metropolitan Board of Works began to be exercised about its height, and in 1877 the architect John Whichcord, who had considerable experience with 'tall' buildings, was roped in, gave technical advice, and disclaimed all aesthetic responsibility. Finally, in the Eighties, E. R. Robson was to give Queen Anne's Mansions its most offensive ranges nearest the park. Its ungainly bulk as seen from Tothill Street near Westminster Abbey was the subject of a gloomy drawing by Joseph Pennell published with Henry James's *English Hours*.

More sites in Victoria Street were gradually being taken for 'chambers' and 'mansions', usually a mixture of offices and flats with some shops below. An early use for London of the term 'mansions' for a block of flats had been the naming of Belgrave Mansions on the Marquis of Westminster's estate in Grosvenor Gardens in 1866. This notion might have come from New York, where a 'House of Mansions' had been built in 1855. The ground floor at the west corner of Strutton Ground and Victoria Street from 1869 contained England's first Meteorological Office, founded by Captain Robert Fitzroy of the *Beagle*. Further along on the south side there developed during the Seventies one of London's best clubs, in a sense, the Army & Navy Stores, begun in 1871 as a co-operative venture in buying wine, food and tobacco by members of the forces stationed in London. The position of Victoria Street was suitable, near Wellington Barracks, the Horse Guards, the War Office and clubs in Pall Mall, while to southward yellow-brick buildings now occupied by the Roman Catholic hierarchy but originally built for officials of the New Bridewell, were then occupied by the Guards. But 'the Stores' quickly outgrew its origins to become, in a *palazzo* built for a distillery the decade before, an almost unique institution (if one did not prefer the Civil Service Stores in the Haymarket):

It is about three o'clock in the afternoon, and in the course of a walk from Victoria Station towards the Houses of Parliament, down a long, gaunt street, with huge mansions containing flats, or lawyers' offices, or the chambers of colonial and parliamentary agents, one notices midway, on the right-hand side, rows of carriages and cabs, two or three deep, drawn up in front of a

137

handsome block of buildings. Every kind of vehicle that can be bought or hired in London is here—from the open barouche or closed brougham, with their thoroughbred horses, to the carriage jobbed by the month, or let out by the hour, as well as the hansom or four-wheeler. . . .

The establishment is not only an emporium, but a lounge, a place of gossip and pleasure as well as of business. . . . Around and about . . . are groups of well-dressed buyers, who have been giving orders for every sort of article that their households or drawing-rooms can need. There are many, too, who seem to have no thought of buying anything, or who, if they have fulfilled the object with which they ostensibly came hither, linger on, with no other visible aim than to meet their friends and discuss the news or scandal of the day. . . . The place, in fact, discharges not a few of the purposes of a club for ladies and gentlemen. . . . (T. H. S. Escott, *England*, 1879)

In such a neighbourhood the new flats of Victoria Street had more social *cachet* than before, some taking the place of the town house as *pied à terre* for nobility and gentry, and conveniently near the Houses of Parliament for M.P.s. Toward the end of the Seventies, the block east of Carlisle Place included Lord de l'Isle and Dudley, Blanchard Jerrold (who wrote the text for Doré's *London* plates), and the Earl of Winchilsea and Nottingham. At the beginning of the Seventies, the roster for Albert Mansions opposite included Alfred Tennyson, John Stuart Mill, 'Hon. Henry Graves, artist', and Arthur Sullivan.

As is sometimes forgotten, Gilbert and Sullivan's début together was with *Thespis* on Boxing Day 1871 at the Gaiety Theatre in the Strand (the old Gaiety, replaced by an Edwardian theatre after the making of Aldwych). The hit song of the evening was the *Railway junction song*—the music for which is lost—with 'a screaming, whistling and shouting chorus' (*The Era*) rendering 'the whirl and thunder of a railway train at express speed' (*Sunday Times*), which 'evoked a stormy encore' (*London and Provincial Entr'acte*) and fairly brought down the house. Everybody in the house lived near a railway line.

The best opera box in town, for anyone as fond of the London scene as Henry James, was a seat in a hansom, that vehicle of vantage, spurting or slackening with the current; white ties and dressed heads greeting one another over the aprons of rattling hansoms, in the City seeing St Paul's for the first time over the apron of a hansom ascending Ludgate Hill, in the winter the splashing of hansoms in the Strand with shopfronts shining into the fog, in the Season the vortex at Hyde Park Corner (*English Hours*). The basic mechanism, the horse, he seldom mentioned. No city in history can have been as full of horses as London was in the years just before the internal combustion engine was perfected. They slipped on the ice, they died with the heat, their habits and droppings were facts of life. Cab drivers were part of the scenery too. In 1872 the *Builder* referred to a new thing in Birmingham, a 'Cabmen's Rest', or shelter. By 1875 London's first cabmen's shelter, with large windows, stood in St John's Wood, and by the Eighties the developed version like a little gabled wooden house, with smaller windows for warmth, a ventilator turret on the roof, and room to make coffee within, stood as a few still stand: on Kensington Gore, Hanover Square, Pont Street at Cadogan Place, and Chelsea Embankment near Albert Bridge, and formerly many more (*Fig. 39*). J. C. Dollmann's painting of a cab-stand with one of these shelters is in the London Museum.

Fig. 39 *Lamp standard and cab shelter on Victoria Embankment*

Another perpetual feature of the London scene was the pillar box, periodically altered a bit in design after its introduction in 1855. The hexagonal Penfold type installed between 1866 and 1879 is the most redolent of the Late Victorian scene of its kind, in fact the earliest type surviving in London although earlier ones survive elsewhere in England and the Channel Islands. An architect named J. W. Penfold (for many years surveyor to the Goldsmiths' Company and honorary secretary to the Surveyors' Institution) designed the prototype, slightly modified during the years it was being installed, with its beaded and lotus-covered ball-topped roof on a six-sided body. As of 1964, forty-one of these still stood in London, none of them in central London. As for the bright red colour we now take for granted, London's first letter boxes were a sort of greenish bronze, which must have been almost invisible from a distance in bad weather, but the change to red was decreed in 1874 and completed in 1884 (the whole story is in *The Letter-Box* by J. Y. Farrugia, 1969). The other standard red of our street scene today, the London bus, did not appear until the amalgamation of many companies in this century.

One standard feature of London Thames views was installed in 1878, Cleopatra's Needle (*Fig. 51*). When this ancient obelisk, after a perilous voyage from Egypt, was about to be set up on the Victoria Embankment opposite the foot of old Ivybridge Lane, the Poet Laureate provided at Dean Stanley's request ten lines in its honour, supposedly to be engraved on its new pedestal. But when the pedestal was erected in September it did not, nor does it now, bear Tennyson's lines, that partly run: 'Whence your own citizens, for their own renown,/Through strange seas drew me to your monster town.' It may be that 'for their own renown' (though doubtless referring to London's renown generally) stuck in the throat of Professor Erasmus Wilson, F.R.C.S., who had paid for the obelisk's transport in a philanthropic spirit. Wilson, who was knighted in 1881 on becoming President of the Royal College of Surgeons, was one of the first specialists in skin diseases; his book of 1861 on *The Eastern or Turkish Bath* was instrumental in its introduction to London, signalized by the construction of Turkish baths in 1862 in Jermyn Street and in Victoria Street. Deeply interested in Egyptian archaeology, he contributed to Flinders Petrie's excavations. Skilful investment in gas and railway company shares had brought him wealth, much of which went to charity. And part of it brought this arrogant finger of rock, saying as Tennyson said it did: 'I was when

London was not. I am here.' The Metropolitan Board of Works flanked it with suitable bronze sphinxes, and placed on the Embankment cast iron benches with kneeling camels, all doubtless celebrating the English presence at Suez. The pedestal bears marks of bombardment from the 1939–45 war, and the Thames at high tide slaps about its steps.

The philanthropic spirit helped to save some of London's green space, too. The whole question of public rights to ancient common lands had been coming to a head at a time of intense demand for building land. Wandsworth Common had been much diminished by railways and a grasping Lord of the Manor. Hampstead Heath was saved from its Lord of the Manor by nearby tenants powerful enough to fight the Private Bills he kept attempting to put through Parliament to enable him to turn it into a building estate; after his death, the Metropolitan Board of Works was enabled by the Hampstead Heath Act of 1871 to buy up all the manorial rights and dedicate the Heath to the public. Tooting Common was rescued from developers by two rich neighbours who were able and willing to swoop in and buy it in 1868 without the delay of more official procedures, and quietly hold it until the MBW could buy it from them in 1873 for exactly the same sum, £10,200, after a good deal of local controversy. One of the two men was the Australia merchant Philip Flower of Furzedown (where a College of Education now occupies his house). The other was Beriah Drew of Streatham, whose firm in Blackman Street, Southwark, had specialized in cod-liver-oil-with-quinine during the cholera epidemics, a thought to savour on Tooting Common. These and other entirely open, wild spaces obtained for public use at around the same time are among the glories of London.

In London's far north, Alexandra Palace sprawls along its ridge like a stranded dinosaur. It looks south-east over Hornsey towards another ridge that reaches east from Highgate and obscures most of central London save the top of St Paul's dome, but with a vast sweep of view eastward. Originally built with materials from the 1862 Exhibition as a northern counterpart to the Sydenham Crystal Palace, opened with much fanfare in 1873 and almost immediately burned down, it was rebuilt and reopened in 1875, a pleasure palace too expensively and hugely planned to work. Its yellow and white bricks with cement dressings have gone khaki, three ridiculously elongated pavilion roofs have gone, and the pipes of the marvellous Willis organ lie in store. Various uses are made of its vast halls, and

Fig. 40 *St Augustine, Kilburn, Lady Chapel in 1896*

the terrace is a fine place to sit especially when the bar is open. Even if the Ally Pally's indomitable builders and rebuilders made an, in a way, admirable miscalculation, it wouldn't make a splendid or a poignant ruin.

Churches when fully vaulted—that is, with clearly articulated skeletons—can make splendid, poignant ruins (as Renaissance painters knew when they used ruins as haunting stage sets for Madonnas). Among the many churches ruined by the last war was Pearson's Gothic St John the Evangelist, Red Lion Square (west side) in Holborn. Rebuilding at first seemed possible, but ruin was further compounded by human agencies, so its fine fractured structure was tidied away. Nevertheless there remain three other churches around London designed by Pearson in the same re-creative spurt in the Seventies: the sort of re-creation that consists in re-thinking and re-feeling old elements and amounts to creation. These are St Augustine, Kilburn Park Road; St Michael, Poplar Walk in Croydon; and St John the Evangelist, Sylvan Road, Upper Norwood. Even the smaller space of the Lady Chapel at Kilburn (which was a Tractarian, or Anglo-Catholic, foundation) is fully vaulted, with glass and wall-painting by the well-known church furnishers Clayton & Bell (*Fig. 40*). As for the great naves of these churches, and the earlier St Peter, Vauxhall (p. 114), Pearson's soaring stone-ribbed vaults give a sense of rock-based, exalted faith as the hymns of that period do: *The Church's one foundation, Onward Christian soldiers* (which became more especially associated with the new Salvation Army), *For all the saints* with 'their rock, their fortress and their might', and *Through the night of doubt and sorrow* with its sense of triumphant pilgrimage. There was no distinction in structural splendour between provision for the suburban well-to-do at Upper Norwood and for the crowded new parish in Holborn, but an analysis of the types of people contributing to and attending each at first in the Seventies might reveal differences in expectations. And there is irony in Pearson's and other architects' attainment of serene rocklike form for the Church of England just as it was entering a time of doubt.

CHAPTER SIX

The Eighties: Outcast London, Baedeker's London

During this decade central London struggled with slums, courted tourists, and thrust striking roofs above the Thames skyline. Restaurants, theatres and music halls multiplied. And two more thoroughfares then being carved through the central mass offered the worst architectural fare yet—mere cab-routes, some outspoken critics said. But at least and at last the surgery required to make Shaftesbury Avenue and Charing Cross Road was being done on the basis that slum clearance meant rehousing the displaced inhabitants: the Metropolitan Board of Works was not authorized. to build for them, but acquired and cleared properties which it then disposed of to private developers who were obliged to build for them. This obligation, incorporated in the Act of 1877 authorizing the new streets, resulted in the large-scale meanness of Sandringham Buildings (1883–4), two grimly facing rows that dominate the Charing Cross Road south of Cambridge Circus. Unnecessarily grim they were and are, yet they housed 900 people in mainly three-room tenements on the site of an area formerly 'a veritable focus of every danger which can menace the health and social order of a city' (Superintendent of Police to Home Secretary, 1882). Eventually the booksellers who set up shop on the ground floors of Sandringham Buildings came to mean 'Charing Cross Road' to bookbuyers everywhere. Shaftesbury Avenue, excepting some of its theatres, was from Cambridge Circus westward in the hands of fifth-rate architects, for example much of the south side by the firm of Martin & Purchase. Small-scale meanness was their speciality, in what might be called the 'stuffed-pediment' style of cement ornament served with red brick. (The full before-and-after story of these two thoroughfares can be found in the *Survey of London*.)

Fig. 41 *Potential slum: court in Lambeth, photograph c. 1860 by W. Strudwick*

There were various sorts of slums but a basic trait they had in common was bad circulation (*Fig. 41*). The 'art of close building', as one medical officer called it, usually stopped circulation where that had been poorly planned from the start or where it had been planned for a tenth or a fiftieth of the number of people that accumulated. A mews cul-de-sac approached through one inconspicuous arched entry for the horses stabled there, with perhaps smaller pedestrian entries from yards or beside the yards of premises that backed on to the stables, was one classic potential site for a slum. Horace Street, Marylebone, was one of those, its name temporarily changed from Cato Street after the conspirators of 1820 were caught over a stable there: a fairly new neighbourhood in 1820, but black slum by the time Charles Booth mapped it at the end of the Eighties. Compton Place on the Foundling Estate in Bloomsbury was another, with houses back-to-back on a series of undrained courts opening out of it, all erased in the Eighties (as described by Donald Olsen in his *Town Planning in London*, 1964).

In St Marylebone from the mid-Sixties Octavia Hill had been engaged upon her own private, practical, almost single-handed campaign against the slum-pockets behind genteel streets. A typical warren lay behind the west side of Marylebone High Street below Paddington Street, along the east edge of what was then a disused burial ground, now a public garden. There Miss Hill made her first venture as landlord in Paradise Place, now Garbutt Place, gradually reconditioning three houses bought for her by Ruskin. After that, although housing management not rebuilding was her primary interest, she had the assistance of an architect, Elijah Hoole, for over forty years. One black spot brightened and partly rebuilt by her was the court she renamed St Christopher's Place, running south from Wigmore Street and connected with Oxford Street by Gee Court, the sort of alleys where pre-Victorian shop assistants once lived and where a vicious slum population had accumulated. On one of the gabled minimal-Gothic blocks Hoole built there for Octavia Hill (west side near the north end) is a plaque saying 'St Christopher's Place 1877' and above it a figure of the saint in a niche, said to have been designed for her by William Morris. Today expensive antiques are sold in St Christopher's Place.

Octavia Hill described her work in a series of articles in the *Fortnightly* and *Macmillan's Magazine*, republished in 1875 as a book, *Homes of the London Poor* (reprinted 1970). Private effort, this practical landlady clearly saw, was not enough: 'There are courts beyond courts of the worst kind, in the East-end especially,' she said, 'where there is not a vestige of a title which would warrant any society or individual in erecting a substantial building.' Confusion over land ownership, and so over responsibility for what sat on the land, was a cardinal slum trait. Octavia Hill's reports and the agitation they caused helped to bring about legislation authorizing the sort of clearance by a public authority that was done to make Shaftesbury Avenue and Charing Cross Road. All that was under way before the renewed and noisier agitation set off in 1883 when a group of Congregational ministers published a fighting pamphlet, *The Bitter Cry of Outcast London*. The public at large heard of it when this was republished to a much wider audience by the *Pall Mall Gazette*. This was followed by an article in the November *National Review* calling for action, by the leader of the Conservative party, Lord Salisbury (a bit of a slum landlord himself: the decaying alleys of Ryder's Court just off the north-east corner of Leicester Square, on the Salisbury Estate, were only replaced by Daly's Theatre after 1889; but Ryder's Court was a tiny drop in London's bucket of trouble). *Punch* immediately published Tenniel's bitter drawing, *Mammon's Rents*, of the house-jobber's rent-collector getting him his '50 to 60 per cent. upon his money', quoting *The Bitter Cry*, and with bitter verses sounding like *Punch* of the Forties only more so (10 November 1883). London was Satan's 'branch-Hades' (November 17), 'the House that Capital built!' (with Tenniel's drawing of the President of the Local Government Board 'seeing for himself' in Clerkenwell, December 1); and then the inevitable 'Very Latest Craze' in high society, 'Lord Archibald is going to take us to a dear little Slum he's found' (December 22). The result of *The Bitter Cry* was a Royal Commission, on which the Prince of Wales, Cardinal Manning, Lord Salisbury and others sat, and this led to the Housing of the Working Classes Act of 1890, greatly widening the powers of local authorities. By then there was a County of London, with an elected Council superseding the old Metropolitan Board of Works.

Another result of *The Bitter Cry* was Charles Booth's monumental *Life and Labour of the People in London*, begun with a study of Tower Hamlets published in 1887. Booth's seventeen-volume work was in three series: on Poverty, classifying London neighbourhood by neighbourhood at seven levels down to 'vicious, semi-criminal', with maps first made in 1889; on Industry, trade by trade beginning with the builders (published 1895); and finally on Religious Influences, based on a census of church and chapel attendance made by Booth and his helpers at the end of the century. For anyone caring to know more about the fabric of Late Victorian London, the section on the building trades is essential 'by nature of the product'. Modern abridgements of the whole seventeen volumes fail to convey the cumulative effect of Booth's vision of London's variousness. He saw Late Victorian poverty and industry and religion in their local context. 'Each district has its character,' he said, 'its peculiar flavour. One seems to be conscious of it in the streets. It may be in the faces of the people, or in what they carry—perhaps a reflection is thrown in this way from the prevailing trades—or it may lie in the sounds one hears, or in the character of the buildings.'

Some of this flavour survives in the glass plates of old photographers. Boiled down to the modern printed page, a little is left: *Fig. 42* is a view of Fetter Lane in about 1880, just before seven buildings on

147

the west side between Norwich Court and Greystoke Place gave way to one flavourless warehouse. Right to left, they were Hooke the baker in premises of about 1790, Twite the greengrocer in a late-medieval house, the Congregational chapel of about 1820, a printing works of perhaps 1840, coffee rooms and the Vintners' Arms both in Georgian premises—in sum, very little of it Victorian-built and lacking for us the flavour of smells and bustle, but part of the scenery of four decades of Victorian life and just on the point of losing its composite character. In other streets, of course, saltless rows of Georgian fronts were in the process of replacement by highly flavoured fronts of extremely individual character.

One aspect of character that faded in this period was the formerly distinctive dress of building workmen, as of Tenniel's Carpenter for *Through the Looking-Glass*: 'The brown-paper cap, the moleskin or corduroy trousers, with a rule-pocket from which a portion of the rule stood out, and the apron . . . of the carpenter, joiner and other woodworkers', the leather aprons of masons and bricklayers. Skilled artisans, complained the *Builder* in 1879, were hard to identify, so completely had they 'thrown off the once distinctive signs of their ancient callings . . . but your modern building workman is a gentleman . . . and does not care to exhibit any of the signs of his trade outside the workshop'. One wonders ·if mass public transport to work beyond a man's own neighbourhood had something to do with it.

Building workmen in whatever garb had been swarming over the new Law Courts, on the site of wretched slums north of the Strand, during most of the Seventies. The architect, Street, died in 1881 before work was finished, worn out with official hectoring and the parsimony of an unsympathetic Government, and leaving behind him London's last great Gothic Revival building. Its translation of thirteenth-century France into Portland stone was as out of date for the taste of 1880 as the Houses of Parliament had been for the taste of 1860, when Barry too died untimely after years of trial under the Government of his day. Because of Portland stone's retention of its whiteness wherever the wind and the rain can reach it, a pavement view of the Law Courts' turrets always has the slightly unreal hue of story book illustration. The great vaulted central hall inside is very grand indeed.

As we have seen, the first of the palatial restaurants appeared in the Seventies. The Criterion, with its theatre in the basement, on Piccadilly Circus and, next to the Gaiety Theatre in the Strand, the

Fig. 42 *Fetter Lane, west side above Greystoke Place, about 1880*

Gaiety Restaurant with its Gothic sort of front (probably influenced by St James's Hall and its restaurant), had both been started by a firm of wine merchants and caterers, Spiers & Pond. Conan Doyle's very first Sherlock Holmes story, *A Study in Scarlet*, written about 1885, begins in the Criterion Bar—probably the Long Bar with its glistering gold ceiling—and continues over lunch at the Holborn Restaurant. The rebuilding of that former casino by Archer & Green of the Café Royal had just been completed in 1883, and contemporary descriptions wallowed in alabaster, rich marble dadoes, gilded Corinthian capitals, Venetian mirrors, and 'electroliers throughout'. Stained glass windows and balcony fronts of brass and ormolu were provided by Messrs Clayton & Bell, more

149

usually thought of as church furnishers (rituals, all sorts, catered for). Messrs Maple did the furniture including carved ebony and walnut screens, and Messrs Doulton made the grill room's ornamental faience.

There had been earlier and more modest restaurants. In the Sixties, young City clerks for whom the old chop-houses were too expensive, too old-fashioned, or too crowded with their betters, could take their midday meal at 'luncheon bars and *restaurants*' (in italic then). A discussion as to whether the food served in these places was worth their prices prompted one elderly merchant to say: '*I* never went to a *restaurant*. When I was young I took my dinner to the office in my pocket, and now I take it in a little bag. They never fleeced me!' Said a commentator in the *Contemporary Review* (December 1868): 'But London clerks are often gentlemen with patent-leather boots and very high pretensions; difficult to please in the matter of beef or fowl, and very punctilious about the finger glasses and rose water. Really . . . when the dinner is provided at a cost of 2s. it seems reasonable'; and still in 1879, according to Baedeker, 'dinner from the joint' cost two shillings in Fleet Street. The elaborate new Holborn Restaurant was not expensive either: six courses, with music, cost three-and-six and so it did still in 1888 (Pascoe, *London of To-day*) and in 1892 (Baedeker). A man could take his family—wife, governess, four children—to the Holborn's Grill Room to lunch for a total bill of fifteen shillings in 1888. For couples dining out, before the theatre or just for a change, hotels now competed with restaurants by opening their dining rooms to non-residents. Both the family luncheon and the dining-out meant a whole new set of social habits.

Not only were there more people than ever in London—the term Greater London was now being used—but more of them were moving about, in search of shopping, in search of entertainment, and more of the moving about was by public transport. People flocked to exhibitions held alongside the open gardens between the Albert Hall and the Natural History Museum until 1887, when plans for the Imperial Institute began; thereafter, exhibitions were held both at Earl's Court and at Olympia, and people still flocked to the Crystal Palace. Music halls and theatres flourished more than ever. Leicester Square and Piccadilly Circus already formed a nucleus of night life, with the Empire, the Alhambra, the Pavilion and all the satellite night spots.

The Empire had a complicated history before its opening under that name in 1884 (*Fig. 43*). Its narrow front on the north side of Leicester Square was and is the width of the five-window front of the house built there in 1683, the area behind it greatly expanding over the years from that of the original stable-yard. In 1880 a French company started a circular structure there for a panorama showing the Charge of the Light Brigade, but was supplanted in 1882 by a theatre eventually opening as the Empire, after passing through the hands of a series of architects including Verity of the Criterion, but apparently retaining not only part of the circular shell but the entrance front designed by some obscure Frenchman in 1880. That was the old Empire front of 1914-war nostalgia, with a great arched window framed by a pediment on pairs of pilasters, all replaced in 1927 by a rather good modern-classical front that still lurks behind the electric signs. The old auditorium set in the panorama shell on a north–south axis was replaced in 1927 by a larger cinema on an east–west axis. Part of Verity's plans were the wide promenades behind the old Empire's seats, famous for their *demi-*

Fig. 43 *Empire Theatre when it opened in 1884*

mondaine life. Shakespeare on his marble pedestal in Grant's garden has been contemplating the Empire's public ever since they opened the place.

On Shakespeare's right on the east side of Leicester Square was the Alhambra in its building of the Fifties (*Fig. 38*), made originally for the Royal Panopticon of Science and Art, until that was burned down in a spectacular fire in 1882 (whereupon a special benefit performance of the new Savoy opera *Iolanthe* was given to help the Alhambra actors, with of course extra applause for the Fairy Queen's ode to the very real Captain Shaw of the Fire Brigade; people still remember hearing their parents tell how the splendid captain took a bow from his seat in the stalls). The new building incorporated the old front and some of the Saracenic ironwork left inside, but the whole thing gave way in the 1930s to the Odeon cinema. The great days of both the Alhambra and the Empire were the thirty years before 1914. The circulation of crowds in and out of the Square, first made possible with new exits and entrances through New Coventry Street and New Cranbourn Street in the Forties, was further stirred in the Eighties by the construction of Charing Cross Road and Shaftesbury Avenue to eastward and northward.

Victorian London never lacked visitors as we have seen, especially for the great exhibitions and for the coronation that more and more people in the Eighties knew only by hearsay. Baedeker's guide 'to the greatest city in the modern world' already existed in German, and in 1877 the first edition in English was published, modestly forbearing from any attempt at 'an exhaustive account of so stupendous a city'. The selected short-list of hotels occupied three pages (1879 edition). Claridge's, still in a series of altered Georgian houses, maintained its patronage 'chiefly by royalty and the nobility . . . the first hotel in London . . . very expensive'. Strangers were 'cautioned against going to any unrecommended house near Leicester Square'. Morley's Hotel in Trafalgar Square was 'pleasantly situated, and much frequented by Americans'. There were many quiet family hotels in the streets leading from the Strand to the Thames Embankment. And there were the big station hotels. During the Eighties, Northumberland Avenue boasted not only the Grand but the Metropole and the Victoria, of similar architectural quality. Not continuously successful as hotels, these were nevertheless wonderfully situated near theatres, restaurants, shops, Westminster, and the river. If today they were rescued from office use and turned into multi-celled super-hostels for tourists and students, how much more sightseeing in the central area such travellers could do on foot, without the present invasion by motor-coaches.

The best new hotel of the Eighties was the Savoy, built for D'Oyly Carte beside his new Savoy Theatre of 1881 (1878–89 was the great period of the nine Gilbert & Sullivan operas from *Pinafore* to *The Gondoliers*). Arthur Mackmurdo was concerned in the hotel's design (the river block; Collcutt's Strand block was later) and it had Morris wallpapers, De Morgan tiles, more bathrooms than any English hotel had ever had before, and electric lights throughout. (The fact that yellow became a more generally fashionable colour in the Eighties and Nineties may have had something to do with the new tones of electric light; yet designers like Godwin, inspired by Japanese prints and bamboo furniture, were already using yellow in interior decoration in the Seventies.) From the Savoy in 1896 Whistler was to make eight lithographs of the Thames, poignant nocturnes in grey; and there Monet was to paint during three visits at the turn of the century a long series of impressions of Waterloo Bridge, the Charing Cross railway bridge, and once more the haunting skyline he had painted in 1871, the Houses of Parliament. The Savoy stands almost at the head of the great arc of the Thames between London Bridge and Lambeth Bridge. Its view now includes the Shell Building on the opposite shore.

On a very different level of creation, the building of hotels—or the sort of block that might be altered from flats or a club to a hotel or offices without too much trouble—was attracting speculators of various shades of grey. To one really inspired crop of rascals, London owed the Hotel Cecil (architects Perry & Reed, who rebuilt the Alhambra) and the Hyde Park Hotel in Knightsbridge (designed as Hyde Park Court by Archer & Green of the Holborn Restaurant), among several other structures they raised during the Eighties and Nineties by a wonderful campaign of high finance. Behind it were eight 'companies' that shared offices and all owed one another money, swapping assets when the accountants came round and engaging in the kind of improvisation that sounds more like the Marx Brothers (and is best described by Peter Ferriday as 'The Jabez Balfour Story' in the *Architectural Review* in 1968). Their last speculation, the Cecil or 'Balfour's Folly', did not open until 1896, after its principal backers had been tried and sentenced for multiple frauds. Rising blatantly above its neater neighbour the Savoy, the Cecil was one of the last of the mansarded monsters begotten at Paddington in the Fifties, its twin domes a late rude echo from the Gros-

Fig. 44 *National Liberal Club in 1887*

venor (rebuilt in this century for Shell-Mex). Meanwhile, a speculator of a purer shade whom we have met before, Jonathan Carr of Bedford Park, had bobbed up in 1883 to begin the most spectacular building group of the Eighties, Whitehall Court ('a Palace of Flats') and, attached to one end of it, the National Liberal Club. Two sets of architects, Archer & Green for the former, Waterhouse for the latter, and their general *château* style and stone facing, were Carr's choice. However devoted he was to domestic brickwork, the example of Queen Anne's Mansions was probably enough to prevent its use here on what was Crown property. Two years later, Carr was in trouble, doubtless because he was also developing the site of Baron Grant's house as Kensington Court at the time, so he sold out to one of Jabez Balfour's companies which was able to finish the job. The National Liberal Club, with the once exciting staircase in its tall oval corner tower, was opened in 1887 (*Fig. 44*). And the romantic roofs of Whitehall Court became the most exciting ingredient in the view from St James's Park, rearing up behind the Horse Guards—although the final ingredient, the cupolas of the War Office, were not thrust up between them until after 1900. So, for sheer excitement of one sort or another, London owes much to the Balfour Group of Companies, as it would now be called.

Excitement never did reign in Victoria Street, and some of its sites were still empty. At about the time *Iolanthe* opened in 1882, Arthur Sullivan (knighted 1883) moved his bachelor quarters along the north side to a new block of flats opposite the Army & Navy Stores. Queen's Mansions (not to be confused with Queen Anne's) was a rather stark building for its time, with a murky history suggesting that its almost Chicago School plainness derived from the penny-pinching of a series of speculators, not from Pevsnerian pioneers. Gilbert, on the other hand, chose to settle in Harrington Gardens, off Gloucester Road in South Kensington, where a row of gaily gabled red houses like a light opera set arose to the design of Ernest George, as if for a first act opening on a quay at Ghent (*Fig. 45*). The Flemish note, or 'Low-Country Picturesque', of modish new houses in the Eighties followed the English seventeenth-century notes of the Seventies. George was also responsible for the Albe-

Fig. 45 *Harrington Gardens, W. S. Gilbert's house left centre*

marle Hotel of 1883, now an office building, in salmon-coloured terracotta on Piccadilly facing down St James's Street. (Whistler's etching of that view in 1878 was done from a window of the previous building on the site.) Charles Booth reported that the use of all-over terracotta in London had been attributed to a masons' strike in 1878, but as we have seen the London atmosphere had provoked interest in impervious materials in the Sixties, and influential architects like Waterhouse had been using such materials for some time: after the Natural History Museum came his tomato-coloured Prudential Assurance in Holborn—part of the present building— and the shop at the Bond Street corner of Piccadilly in red and buff. Waterhouse's impervious exteriors have a rather hard appearance, whereas the salmon terracotta work designed by George and later by Collcutt seems a natural outcome of soft-pencil drawings. But Thomas Edward Collcutt was an architect who 'could make picturesqueness dignified', as his obituary by a fellow architect was to put it. This he did in the Imperial Institute (*Fig. 46*).

The short history of that temple of Empire on the former

Fig. 46 *The Imperial Institute*

Horticultural Gardens at Kensington is this: inspired by the Colonial Exhibition of 1886 and the impending Jubilee of 1887, the Government held a limited competition with six invited entrants and Collcutt's winning design was published on the fiftieth anniversary of the Queen's accession; a press view was held in June 1892 and the Queen opened the building in May 1893. As Victorian architectural competitions went, impressively simple. Built to contain exhibition galleries, library, reception and conference rooms, emigration offices, laboratories and sample rooms for Empire products, the Imperial Institute was later used by the University of London but did not long survive the Empire, and is now wholly demolished save for the great central tower—left to 'speak to the centuries' as the Poet Laureate told it to. The amalgam of French, Flemish and Spanish styles Collcutt chose for his language (Esperanto?) was an odd way of expressing the Empire, yet that is an over-literal objection to a most architectural sublimation of 'styles'. The whole was a wonderful structure of Portland stone with a little banding of red brick and sparing use of delicate ornament, with a dramatic staircase inside, and three towers. The green-capped white central tower can be seen from many parts of London still but is rooted in a new lawn. The Imperial Institute was one of those long symmetrical buildings that never look symmetrical except from the air, but it 'grouped well' from any standpoint—whereas one like Pennethorne's University of London building in Burlington Gardens (now part of the British Museum) might make a fine opera set if we could just step back from it centrally enough, but we don't find ourselves happily accepting whichever view of it we do happen to strike in its narrow situation. Collcutt had rediscovered how Barry in the Houses of Parliament, and to a lesser extent Street in the Law Courts, made picturesqueness dignified.

Meanwhile another event of the Golden Jubilee year made darkness visible and misery vocal: the mass socialist demonstration in defence of free speech in Trafalgar Square in November, remembered as Bloody Sunday. Processions converged on the Square from several directions, doubtless the first such use of the new Charing Cross Road, linked to the most direct route from the northern railway stations. The usual English way of containing demonstrations was perhaps better served by the old muddle of non-thoroughfares, as opposed to Haussmann's view of such matters in Paris. That day the police called in the Army and two men in the crowd were killed. Both of London's rallying grounds for free speech have been fought

Fig. 47 *The Pool of London, 1888, by Vicat Cole. View looking upstream to the Tower, London Bridge and St Paul's, before the building of Tower Bridge*

for: there had been the Reform Bill riot of 1866 in Hyde Park, at the north-east edge that we call 'Speakers' Corner'.

A new building for the Metropolitan Police was the last great work of the Eighties, New Scotland Yard by Norman Shaw. For the prominent site by the Thames Embankment near Westminster Bridge, a National Opera House was for a while intended, and an eminent opera-singer 'laid the first brick' in 1875. That project, which journalists called 'Mr Mapleson's famous Opera House, so long a thorn in the side of the Metropolitan Board of Works' (it probably had the vices and graces of Queen Anne's Mansions), was soon suspended and then abandoned as totally unworthy of the site. When rebellious crowds poured into Trafalgar Square in November 1887, the police charged around the corner from Old Scotland Yard. Preparations were then under way for the new building, Shaw's fine main block. (To this, somewhat against his own judgment, he was required to add the south block at the end of his life.) New Scotland Yard is a Late Victorian donjon-keep in stone-banded brick, with brave tourelles translated from the dour turrets of Millbank Prison just upriver, and gables crowned with virile symbols, obelisks sprouting from pediments. (Nobody seemed to mind virility symbols, Victorians being tougher than we think.) Here in this genial fortress the Metropolitan Police had a boldly representative building where, as at Dance's Newgate Prison, the abstract power of the Law impressed wrongdoers and passers-by alike. Now, having outgrown the space, the police offices are housed in an anonymous new skyscraper off Victoria Street which symbolically reduces policemen to drones in any office hive. Meanwhile, their former headquarters ought to be given some other powerful use—even stripped of the second Shaw block if necessary, which would reveal the spirited grandeur of the main block as Victorian wrongdoers and proud policemen saw it.

Downriver, the nearest bridge to the sea was still London Bridge. Below-bridge in the Pool, busiest of river reaches, lay vessels from the ports of the world, alongside Essex barges bringing hay for London horses. Vicat Cole's large canvas (*Fig. 47*) shows the Pool as Joseph Conrad first knew it.

CHAPTER SEVEN

The Nineties: Imperial Image, Poets' Image

While the Imperial Institute's main tower slowly rose to its full height—at two feet a week and without external scaffolding—in 1892, the South Kensington complex of official buildings was still incomplete. Along the western border ran an avenue of mansions, Queen's Gate. To northward there was an undistinguished new red building for the Royal College of Music, and south-eastward the South Kensington Museum waited for vast new extensions; a competition had been held in 1891, but work was not begun until 1899, when its name was changed to the Victoria and Albert Museum. The Imperial Institute itself, however handsome the building, was by 1897 regarded as a failure so far as its imperial purposes were concerned, being thought too far from Parliament and Whitehall. If London was the most 'Imperial-minded' city, as a journalist put it in 1895, it was so minded in practical offices in Whitehall and Lombard Street: South Kensington was museum-minded, education-minded.

The Whitehall area was not yet as we know it, when Gladstone returned to Downing Street for the last time. (The Prime Minister actually lived at No. 10 since Disraeli in 1877 had revived the custom, dropped in 1834, of making his home in the official residence.) South of Scott's Government office building, which faced the whole width of Whitehall as now, two parallel streets lined with little old buildings ran to Parliament Square, a narrow Parliament Street and a narrower King Street. The site of the latter is entirely absorbed in that of the Edwardian Government building now at the corner of the Square. Traffic surging around Parliament Square from Victoria Street or surging over Westminster Bridge to jockey for entry into this delta had been raising doubts about King Street for some time. The Square itself had a smaller green than now, surrounded by an elaborate iron fence. Opposite Downing Street the dignified pavilion roofs of Montagu House stood before the vapours of the river, and north of Montagu House were the eighteenth and early nineteenth-century houses of Whitehall Gardens, some still occupied as private houses, others by clubs or Government ministries. Inigo Jones's Banqueting House had been serving as a Royal Chapel until 1890, when it was turned over to the United Service Institution for use as a museum. North of that, small buildings faced Whitehall all the way to Trafalgar Square, which had remained the same since the entry of Northumberland Avenue; behind the south-west side was still the little neighbourhood of Spring Gardens, much of which was to disappear for the grand entry from the Mall, Admiralty Arch, just before the First World War. The London County Council had taken over the Metropolitan Board of Works' headquarters in Spring Gardens when the Nineties began.

Fig. 48 *Traffic at the Bank*

In the City, the knotted tangle of streets that we know as 'the Bank' was still quietly dominated by Soane's grand one-storey Bank of England (*Fig. 48*). Even though some of its neighbours were taller, the average building height here at one of the world's busiest intersections was unusually low. One Gothic interloper stood up to the classic porticoes of the Mansion House and the Royal Exchange, the office building (now Mappin & Webb) by J. & J. Belcher marking the opening of Queen Victoria Street at the beginning of the Seventies. The open courtyard of the Royal Exchange was now glazed over. The world's first electric-traction tube railway, the City & South London Railway to Stockwell, tunnelling under King William Street had come up under St Mary Woolnoth church, where a former entrance to the crypt became one of the world's first Tube entrances.

Piccadilly Circus, since Shaftesbury Avenue had been brought into it, was no longer a circus but 'a distorted isochromal triangle'

Fig. 49 *Shaftesbury Memorial Fountain, Piccadilly Circus, in 1893*

according to the sculptor Alfred Gilbert. His bronze Shaftesbury Memorial Fountain, crowned with the aluminium figure immediately christened Eros by the newspapers (*Fig. 49*), was completed in the summer of 1893 (the whole story is told in the *Survey of London*, vol. 31). While some critics praised the fountain for its elegance and the *Daily Telegraph* thought it a most promising new departure for public statuary, others were crudely unkind, said it was ludicrous, and so forth. And *Punch*, of course, showed Eros's missing arrow in the back of a passing cabdriver (21 October 1893). The fountain was, perhaps, the world's first permanent outdoor Art Nouveau sculpture, even before that term was born with Bing's shop in Paris in 1895. Whatever the origins of the formal theme in the life of that great friend of the poor, Lord Shaftesbury, the artist has most delicately contrived a series of variations on the letter S. Although the water in such an enclosed and windy space could never make a lavish show as Gilbert hoped it would, the modest flow sliding over his fishy platter does make the bronze come alive—and the silvery rushing figure (when recently scrubbed) needs no such aid. The flower-sellers who used to cluster round the basin are now replaced by 'flower children' and tourists. Whatever the future of Piccadilly Circus, the present traffic-jams do at least give bus-passengers a chance to contemplate one of the world's most beautiful fountains. The surrounding dwarf-wall shown in our early photograph was removed in 1894. Other early and more permanent manifestations in the photograph are the giant advertisements on buildings behind the fountain.

For all the demolitions to make new avenues and bigger buildings, London still had a network of ancient courts and yards, not quite slums, where various branches of the book trade had taken root. Three of these once busy backwaters till partly extant are Took's Court, Racquet Court, and Warwick Court; a vanished fourth was Belle Sauvage Yard. This last was an old coaching-inn yard off the north side of Ludgate Hill between Old Bailey and the site of the Fleet Prison, in the noisy shadow of the railway viaduct and bridge of 1863 (p. 93): 'that enormous flat-iron that lies across the chest of Ludgate Hill', the bridge a 'vulgar daubing of brown paint and barbaric gilding', said Walter Thornbury in the first volume of *Old and New London* (continued by Edward Walford and published by Cassell's 1872–8). On the west side of the yard, John Cassell had taken premises in 1851 for his new publishing firm, greatly extended toward Fleet Lane in the Seventies as Cassell, Petter & Galpin.

Until the entire premises were destroyed by enemy action in 1941, editors laboured to the din of steam printing-presses inside while outside 'the locomotives of the London, Chatham & Dover Railway Company whistled, shunted, and dallied to blow off steam': that was young Arthur Quiller-Couch's impression of Cassell's in the Nineties. Now, Sea Coal Lane has been brought round over the site, the trains on the viaduct are electric, and the railway bridge is painted an apologetic blue.

Took's Court is a narrow way bent between Cursitor Street and Furnival (former Castle) Street just east of Chancery Lane, and bordered now partly by the Patent Office, yet it still contains three Georgian houses, Nos 14–16. From about 1829, Charles Whittingham (known to printing historians as 'the nephew'—of Charles Whittingham founder of the Chiswick Press) had his own printing office at No. 21 Took's Court. After 'the uncle's' death in 1840, he also carried on the works at Chiswick and then, after a gap between leases in Took's Court, in 1852 brought all the work back to No. 21 which became the Chiswick Press thereafter. In the early Forties he was instrumental in the revival of Caslon typefaces, and also took up wood-block colour printing. Handsome examples of the latter were the colour plates of the Chapter House floor at Westminster Abbey in Henry Shaw's *Specimens of Tile Pavements* (p. 35), printed in Took's Court in 1858. Meanwhile, Dickens had described the old passage in dark tones as Cook's Court, 'at most times a shady place' where 'smoke, which is the London ivy' had wreathed itself round the nameplates of law stationers. In the sixteen houses occupied in Took's Court in 1867, there were four law stationers and fifteen law writers; by 1897 there were still three law stationers, but not one law writer: the typewriter had arrived.

The colour printer and wood engraver, Edmund Evans, had his premises at the head of Racquet Court, No. 4 (still standing 1972) from about 1851 until the late Nineties, surrounded by the offices of printing-union officials and bookbinders. Here the plates of Birket Foster, Kate Greenaway, Randolph Caldecott, and Walter Crane came from his presses, along with 'yellowbacks' for railway reading. Racquet Court is a cul-de-sac off the north side of Fleet Street between Shoe Lane and Ludgate Circus, until recently lined with late-seventeenth-century houses (two remain) and the Early Victorian-looking No. 4 at the end with its warehouse windows above a (neo?) Georgian-looking shopfront that might have pleased Kate Greenaway.

Warwick Court, a little piecemeal-built pedestrian thoroughfare, runs down from Gray's Inn into High Holborn opposite the top of Chancery Lane. The *Civil Engineers' and Architects' Journal,* an influential periodical before the *Builder* got into its stride, had its office at No. 13. In the Nineties, the recently founded (and now flourishing) London Topographical Society had a room at No. 8. At No. 3 in the Forties to Sixties was a J. R. Jobbins, also of Westminster, a map surveyor and draughtsman whose name sometimes appears on the surviving estate plans of suburban developers, or on engraved prospectus-views issued to catch charitable subscribers to new dispensaries for the poor; he was printer and engraver for one of the many sets of plates that helped to propagate the Gothic Revival, *Ancient Domestic Architecture* (1858–63), from drawings by Pugin's pupil F. T. Dollmann. By 1867, among the lithographers and map engravers in Warwick Court there was a 'photographic copying company'. By the Nineties, photographic processes and new machines had made themselves felt in every one of these ancient corners.

Partly because of the greater number of photographs taken and surviving, we know more about the Nineties than we do about the rest of the Victorian period. The picture-postcard industry was born soon after 1894, when private cards using adhesive stamps like letters were at last allowed in addition to the plain Government-embossed type of card. It seems likely that the first spate of cards with London views came in the Diamond Jubilee year to provide souvenirs for vast numbers of visitors—as Tallis had issued his first 'street views' in the Coronation summer of 1838. A large proportion of the view-cards issued up to 1914 and even after, show London and environs much as they were in the Nineties. A reverberation of London life, echoing Victorian themes even after 1901, can be felt in the neglected messages often to be found on the backs of those old postcards: a small selection is given at the end of this book. There was also a spate of London albums in 1897, fixing its 'sights' in grey amber at a point in its history that happened to occur just before the arrival of the motor-car. Yet the motor-car was already launched in England, an Act of 1896 having raised the speed limit for self-propelled vehicles to 12 m.p.h., and a Motor Car Show was held at the Imperial Institute in that year by a few enthusiasts headed by the Prince of Wales.

But public transport in the streets of London by bus, tram and cab was entirely horse-drawn until well after 1901. Cabmen thought

Fig. 50 *Street scenery: shop in the Strand* c. *1890, later removed for Aldwych*

they were losing passengers among businessmen because of wider use of telephones, but they were also losing to the greater numbers and comforts of omnibuses, now upholstered inside like first-class railway carriages and much used by the gentry, while workmen felt more at home on the trams. Experts call the bus of the Nineties a triumph of carriage building, 'probably the lightest and strongest vehicle of its kind in the world' (C. E. Lee, *The Horse Bus as a Vehicle*, 1968). For a description of the horse-bus in motion, the undulled eye and ear of a foreigner are best:

> . . . it rumbles forward with a sound of thunder, and the motion of a steamer when they put the table-racks on . . . it is of barbaric majesty. . . . The procession bears onward whole populations lifted high in the air, and swaying and lurching with . . . elephantine gait . . . the common herd of Londoners of both sexes which it bears aloft seems to suffer a change . . . they are conquering princes . . . looking down upon a lower order of human beings from their wobbling steeps. . . . If ever London has her epic poet,

Fig. 51 *River scenery: the Victoria Embankment from an upper window of the Adelphi* c. *1900*

I think he will sing the omnibus. (William Dean Howells, *London Films*, 1905)

London had, not epic poets, but lyric poets in the Nineties, making counterparts of Gilbert's fountain or Whistler's late nocturnes. Francis Thompson, sleeping on the Embankment, saw his religious visions of angels in the streets, 'the traffic of Jacob's ladder . . . betwixt Heaven and Charing Cross'. William Ernest Henley celebrated the 'Golden City' in Trafalgar Square, at sunset shining 'like an angel-market' with Nelson flaming in the gaze of 'the saluting sun', even the 'dingy dreariness of the picture-place' (National Gallery) taking on a 'luminous transiency of grace', and every frontage (even the Grand Hotel's) full of flickering windows in the glory of a day, not dying, but 'dispersed in wafts and drifts of gold'. London still has sunsets as if by Turner, yet there was a determined romanticism abroad in the Nineties. 'Golden city' London had been called before, but Londoners in the Sixties and Seventies were perhaps less ready to swallow it—for instance, the

Illustrated London News after a snowstorm in January 1871:

But we *are* barbarians, after all. We can make an embankment and a viaduct, and throw railway-bridges over frightful precipices, and lay wires that absolutely beat the sun, and deliver messages before the hour at which they are despatched. But we cannot keep our streets clean. Look at London now. 'The proud, golden city' can hardly dare to return the gaze. We have had a few days of snow, and the metropolis of the world is one foul marsh.

We hear that in the present century sometimes, but without the troops upon troops of horses.

Part of London's sublimity in the eyes of poets and painters was the effect of that overlay of chimney-fed fogs, that varnish of soot from every domestic coal fire and railway engine and factory stack. By making the air fit to breathe we have introduced more light of common day and no longer yearn, like lovers of old dirty varnish on paintings, for the Miltonic scenes fog made. There will always be enough natural river mist here for artistic subtleties, but not the old view from Fleet Street when trains crossed the Ludgate viaduct: 'Vast as is the world below the bridge, there is a vaster still on high, and when trains are passing, the steam from the engine will throw the dome of St Paul's into the clouds . . . a commingling of earth and some far-off mysterious palace,' Samuel Butler thought, adding, 'I am not very fond of Milton, but I admit that he does at times put me in mind of Fleet Street' (preface to *Alps and Sanctuaries*, 1890). To Henry Mayhew in 1849, 'to behold the metropolis without its smoke—with its thousand steeples standing out against the clear blue sky sharp and definite in their outlines [perhaps paraphrasing Wordsworth's 'glittering in the smokeless air'] is to see London as it is not—without its native element'. Standing on the little gallery above the dome of St Paul's, with the vast city below him 'half hid in mist and with only glimpses of its greatness visible', Mayhew thought 'it had a much more sublime and ideal effect from the very inability to grasp the whole of its literal reality'. But Dickens grasped the reality of the native element in his famous description in *Our Mutual Friend* of a rusty black fog 'where the whole metropolis was a heap of vapour charged with muffled sound of wheels, and enfolding a gigantic catarrh'. In the Sixties, too, the British Museum portico's 'black army of outlines passing for gods and goddesses' and the Crimea Monument's 'cluster of charred martyrs' in Waterloo Place persuaded one realist that posterity ought to practise 'total abstinence from profuse ornament' (*Fortnightly*, 1 April 1866).

The London-poetry of the Nineties has been called part of a new cult of artificiality. Yet it was part of a very long stream of poems in praise and fear and awe of the place. Laurence Binyon wrote in wondering praise of 'the far-off hum of the streets . . . the gliding hurry, the endless lights' in the Nineties as Tennyson had written in wondering fear of 'the leagues of lights, and the roaring of the wheels' in the Thirties. And the 'rumble of the tremendous human mill' (Henry James) struck different nerves in the same temperament at different times. The *fin-de-siècle* nerve was touched by London-vignettes, London-moods, like Lionel Johnson's *By the Statue of King Charles at Charing Cross*: 'He triumphs now, the dead,/ Beholding London's gloom.' The personal romanticism of the Nineties must have been an individualist reaction to the public romanticism of the Empire. That grand illusion was at its height for the Diamond Jubilee, just before the Boer War. Fifty years earlier; 'Our physical, moral, and intellectual presence is felt in every region of the globe. . . . They cannot do without us' (the *Illustrated London News* in 1849). Now in 1897 in Kipling's *Recessional*, a young man thought it necessary to warn, 'Lest we forget'. One of London's best buildings had been put up to house what the Poet Laureate had called 'a stately memorial . . . Some Imperial Institute'—which didn't work.

A new home for grand illusions, the picture palace (U.S. movie theatre), was to emerge from the Nineties (see Dennis Sharp, *The Picture Palace*, 1969). In March 1896 a kinetoscope, or cine-matograph, performed at the Empire Theatre while an animatograph was being shown at the Alhambra, and these two theatres in Leicester Square were the first homes of moving pictures in England. The word bioscope, or double-projection, was also used, and an American trade name, biograph, appeared in 1897. (The Biograph, the little picture house near Victoria Station which was the first structure in London built expecially for the purpose, was made from a row of shops in about 1905.)

The architecture of entertainment flourished in the Nineties; in fact, during the whole period from the Seventies up to 1914 much of London's skyline and street scenery was moulded by successful theatre and restaurant architects who also, as we have seen, designed hotels and blocks of flats. Just as, in the Fifties and Sixties, so much skyline had been in the hands of successful church architects. (One feels that if Gilbert Scott had been still going in the Eighties, what a restaurant he would have designed, and justified

Fig. 52 *Elephant and Castle as rebuilt* c. *1898*

it morally too, though one doubts if Archer & Green bothered to do that.) After the boldness of gin palaces in the Thirties, there was a long period when the public house was conservatively stuccoed and pilastered, not in the van of design at all, attracting its public with the enormous lamps, the gilding and mahogany, pioneered in the Thirties, and with the glitter of etched glass. In the Thirties too, theatre architects had made adroit use of a theatrical fancy style and then there was a long period while they went on repeating themselves in a world apart from other designers and not much referred to in the building journals. It was only when there opened, in the last quarter of the century, splendiferous restaurants by superior architects like Verity and clever ones like Archer & Green, and theatres by seasoned specialists like C. J. Phipps (the Lyric, Shaftesbury Avenue; Her Majesty's, Haymarket), that the architecture of entertainment was taken seriously. It became big business. When D'Oyly Carte wished to build a Royal English Opera House (later Palace Theatre) at Cambridge Circus, he employed the Imperial Institute's architect. Much of Collcutt's delicate detail at the Palace Theatre, inside and out, has disappeared. Toward the end of the Nineties, after Collcutt's buildings and Shaw's Scotland Yard, as well as the taste for 'Low-Country Picturesque', had shown the way to stripes again, old public houses like the World's End and the Elephant and Castle (*Fig. 52*) burst forth in bands of brickwork, and 'structural polychromy' had a last fling.

One pair of pub-and-restaurant architects, Treadwell & Martin, made successful use of a flamboyant North European mixture of styles that still stands out here and there, as in the Rising Sun in Tottenham Court Road, or, once so delightful, Scott's Restaurant in Coventry Street at the top of the Haymarket, with its wonderful view of streets from the corner windows on the first floor (a building now debased with red paint outside and honky-tonkery inside). For a different public then, the teashop had arrived. In 1894 the first Lyons opened on the south side of Piccadilly near the Circus; right next door there came Slater's with its once-distinctive ballooning semi-circular glass front, and the Aerated Bread Company was already operating nearby.

London's most successful concert hall, Queen's Hall (*Fig. 53*), opened in 1891 at the top of Regent Street (where St George's

Fig. 53 *Queen's Hall*

Hotel is now). There the famous 'Proms' or Promenade Concerts were inaugurated and carried on until the building was destroyed in 1941. Much of the auditorium was sunk below street level so that the hall shouldn't rise above its neighbours. C. J. Phipps did the technical design, and T. E. Knightley the ornamental design—the old dualism of the railway station. Knightley's most extravagant design of all was not for the entertainment industry but for the Birkbeck Bank in Southampton Buildings off Chancery Lane. Until it was most thoughtlessly torn down in 1965, it had all the colossal columns and assurance of the Sixties rendered in Doulton's new Carrara ware of the Eighties, in peacock-green and creamy shades of brown, with bright tiles inside its great domed banking hall. While its covering material was the latest thing for resisting the London atmosphere, its ornament-encrusted façades were old-fashioned, perhaps because both architect and client were elderly men whose vision had been set by the Sixties or before, and because it was a bank. How it must have horrified the more advanced designers of the day, younger men like Charles Harrison Townsend.

Townsend's vision had been formed, or liberated, in the Seventies and Eighties, that is, he was in his forties in this period when he produced the Bishopsgate Institute and the Whitechapel Art Gallery. These and certain houses by Charles Voysey (still in his thirties), in Kidderpore Avenue in Hampstead and in Bedford Park, and the Mary Ward Settlement (now Centre) in Tavistock Place by Smith & Brewer (aged 29 and 24 respectively) are London buildings of the Nineties that look like the twentieth century to us. We cannot speak of 'styles' in connection with them. (The best short summary of the liberated arts of the Eighties and Nineties is Sir Nikolaus Pevsner's *Pioneers of Modern Design*.) Ruskin in 1884, out of the depths of his own disgusts, had morosely pronounced 'the existing art of England to be the mere effluence of Grosvenor Square and Clapham Junction'. To the bright young men, Ruskin had become a shadow and the new spirit a gust of fresh air.

By the end of the Nineties, in street upon street of inner-suburban red-brick houses unaffected by the enthusiasms of living architects, there had occurred among the builders' patterns an amalgamation: the type called (to its namesake's sorrow) Ruskinian, decorated with bits of Gothic foliage, had taken on bits of Queen-Annery from Bedford Park, balustrades, doings on the gables, and so forth. And often still the stilted window arch started by Cockerell sixty years before (Chapter 2), or walls crusty with Gothic dogtooth might rise to curving gables. Perhaps these were the mixtures Ruskin so loathingly foresaw—yet cheerful enough when well-maintained.

The mass housing of the future was the humanely designed Millbank Estate built at the turn of the century by the London County Council around the perimeter of the former prison site where the Tate Gallery was just completed (to a thoroughly antique design). The Millbank Estate was the culmination of the long history of housing, or rather not housing, London's poor, the turn of a century of change in man's inhumanity to man. How right that it rose beside the late site of a prison that had swallowed up so many, warped by London's slums. Sad memories of the Thames-side fortress itself are exorcised by the life-enhancing contents of the Tate, expecially its great collection of Turners.

In the Nineties some church architecture caught the new spirit abroad in the arts. Holy Trinity, Sloane Street, by John D. Sedding and then Henry Wilson and others, was and is a sumptuous gallery of the arts and crafts of stone and metal and glass. One of London's most prominent religious buildings was begun in the Nineties, the Roman Catholic Westminster Cathedral on the New Bridewell prison site near Victoria Street. Cardinal Wiseman had wanted a great central cathedral, Archbishop as he was of Westminster although enthroned in Southwark; Cardinal Manning had felt that money spent on educating children was more important than money spent on buildings; Cardinal Vaughan finally undertook to commission the architect John Francis Bentley in 1894; both Vaughan and Bentley were dead by the time the building was finished in 1903. The design was based on Byzantine and Early Christian sources as least likely to raise comparisons with either Westminster Abbey or St Paul's. Its tall thin tower had no later rival on the skyline until the Post Office Tower, and its row of shallow saucer domes looks pleasantly foreign. Today's modernists prefer the bare geometry of the unlined domes inside to the marble and mosaics with which the interior is gradually being clothed as intended. (Outside, no one can have intended that neighbouring blocks of flats should now so repetitively mimic the Cathedral's dignified stone banding of its red brickwork by their assertive cream-painted stripes.) The great vessel was obscured from the start by Ashton's Victoria Street flats of forty years before (demolished 1971). It was as if, like early dissenting chapels, this non-Anglican building had to immure itself, however far its tower could be seen.

Fig. 54 *Tower Bridge*

And finally, Tower Bridge (1886–95), though not the last chrono-
logically, was in a sense the last building of the Victorian era. Here
imperial imagery and poets' imagery were fused (*Fig. 54*). Half
suspension bridge and half drawbridge, with its steelwork partly
clothed in Gothic masonry and approached by Gothic gatehouses, it
bestrides 'the Pool' below London Bridge to carry a relief road from
the Minories and East London to Bermondsey and South London.
It had, inevitably, two authors, an architect and an engineer. Sir
Horace Jones, a paunchy bearded man who looked like the Architect
to the City Corporation, was designer of Smithfield, Leadenhall and
Billingsgate Markets and of the griffin that replaced Temple Bar:
he presumably designed the towers and gatehouses of the bridge,
and then he died in 1887. Thereafter it was in the hands of John
Wolfe Barry: born in the year his father won the Houses of Parliament competition, for his first twenty-four years he grew up, as it
were, along with that building. In his late twenties he was resident
engineer under Hawkshaw for the Charing Cross and Cannon
Street railway extensions, and was subsequently concerned with the
Blackfriars railway bridge and station. The Roeblings' Brooklyn

Bridge was completed three years before Tower Bridge was begun, but presumably that great suspension bridge was of no interest here: its great height above the water required approaches much farther inland than was possible in London, on the City side anyway. The modernity of Brooklyn Bridge, like a logical progression from Brunel's suspension bridges, made Tower Bridge look like the series of compromises it was. Young architects of that day despised such clothing of modern machinery in what looked like speculator's hotel-Gothic. The new look of the Nineties with public masonry was rather to be seen at the north entrance to Blackwall Tunnel (by a London County Council architect) in 1897, with its banded turrets like Art Nouveau descendants of Shaw's turrets on Scotland Yard. Yet there is something about Gothic pinnacles and river mist that perhaps a Barry was bound to understand, and the vicinity of the Tower of London was doubtless thought to require a historic style. Walk across Tower Bridge, watch it from a boat or Tower Hill or other bridges: what a piece of scenery! Its full dualism is less well known. The remarkable mechanism is 'the most perfect example of integrated hydraulic power in the world', said a letter to *The Times* (9 December 1971). 'The beam engines in the rooms under the Southwark approach are marvellous objects in their own right. . . . In the river towers the hydraulic engines which move the bascules are wonderful examples of engineering design . . . a complex and interlocking system.' Now that river traffic above-bridge has dwindled so much, by all means let Tower Bridge become a museum of industrial archaeology, and periodically hold up the road traffic, when that is least inconvenient, so that some of the visitors who now flock to watch the Changing of the Guard can flock instead to see the Raising of the Bridge.

No one building could possibly typify the variousness of Victorian London, but a long stream of ideas of the Sublime and the Picturesque is bracketed between the Palace of Westminster and the great bridge at the Tower.

CHAPTER EIGHT

The Fabric of London in 1901 and After

The funeral procession formed at Victoria Station and proceeded to Paddington Station. In 1837, the site of the one had been a Thames backwater busy with barges and lined with wharves, surrounded by former market gardens half-sown with houses; the site of the other, a reservoir beside an arm of the Grand Junction Canal near its link with the Regent's Canal, in a bustling neighbourhood of wharves and warehouses for barge-borne goods. By 1901, Victoria and Paddington had been bustling railway stations for more than forty years.

The gun-carriage bearing the coffin and on it the crown, orb and sceptre, with kings riding after and thick crowds watching silently in the wintry air, proceeded along Buckingham Palace Road past the Palace stables to the Mall, past the Palace gates and the future memorial site, between the Parks to turn left at Marlborough Gate and past the courtyard of the old dark-red palace where the accession of 1837 was proclaimed, up St James's past stone-faced clubs and left into Piccadilly past terracotta-faced hotels, past the black-draped courtyard walls of old Devonshire House and along Green Park to Hyde Park Corner, the daily din reduced to the beat of drums and hooves in slow time, through the Ionic screen beside Apsley House and up the east road of the Park, surveyed from a distance beyond the rows of heads by Park Lane's new South African millionaires' houses, then through the Marble Arch and over the old Tyburn site where two Roman roads once met, a funeral route incredibly old, and up the Edgware Road still bordered by brown-brick houses with taller creamy mansions behind, to turn left and down the length of Sussex Gardens to London Street, and so to Paddington. The royal progress begun with the slow voyage from Cowes through the avenue of ships, and the special train from Portsmouth, ended with the last railway journey to Windsor. (Victoria had been Queen for five years before her first railway journey.) And so the old Queen, Georgian-born in a William-and-Mary suburb, left the Greater Babylon behind her.

The way to Windsor lay through the Middlesex countryside traversed by the coaches of the Archbishop of Canterbury and the Lord Chancellor that early morning in June 1837—a countryside in 1901 not all suburban yet, much of it still the villagey country Cockneys knew best. (It is impossible to study the growth of Greater London without lingering over the shrinkage of the Home Counties; the best analysis of one of them in relation to London is the too-little-known *Middlesex* by Michael Robbins, 1953, the author being most suitably a pillar of London Transport.) Soon after 1901, transport electrified or petrol-powered began to dispense with the need for hay.

Vaster than ever, London was governed at last by one representative elected authority (with still, the Corporation of the City of London embedded in its midst). More slum clearance was already under way for new avenues at Aldwych and Kingsway. There and in the later rebuilding of Regent Street, an Edwardian scale was to swell the heavy white masonry of what has sometimes been called an imperialist classicism, significantly when the firmest optimism of Empire was gone. A very great deal of the Victorian fabric existed until 1940; photographs taken in the 1920s show how much of that fabric then remained even though styles of life had changed, and even though certain large-scale rebuilding interrupted by the First World War continued the Edwardian afflatus. Since 1940, bombardiers and then developers have destroyed with their usual discrimination.

Victorian London was largely made by developers, much of it on land not previously built upon. It is for us to exercise real discrimination by determining which new developments offer something worth the destruction of the old, and which do not. We are rediscovering, for one thing, that what the Early Victorians called street architecture and the more thoughtful Late Victorians called the 'new London's museum of architectural masks' is stimulating to have around (*Figs. 55, 56*). Of London's street scenery one philosopher said in 1873: 'Let us hope that time and circumstance will weld it into some sort of harmony, or that we may, with the variety, be providing for our descendants, if not a feast of beauty for the eye,

N

Fig. 55 *Victorian London inner suburb in 1971 : Elsynge Road, Wandsworth*

plenty of that picturesqueness about which the present generation
talks so much and knows so little' (James Thorne in the *Companion
to the British Almanac for 1874*). In a word, character, which we
neglect and smooth out, like photograph-retouchers, at our peril.
And it will be a poor time for Londoners when they can no longer
hold the splendid Victorian attitude that:

It is the peculiar compensation to the inhabitants of a city like
this, that what others gain from the study and enjoyment of
Nature, you may gain from the study and enjoyment of History.
What geology, mineralogy, and botany are to the dwellers in
rustic parishes, that History is to the occupants of streets, the
neighbours of houses, whose very names are famous . . . even the
commonest streets in London . . . [seeing] there what others see

not; and as the structure of the earth to a student of geology becomes an orderly and beautiful system instead of a disjointed mass of stone and earth, so London, to a student of History, instead of a mere collection of bricks and mortar, becomes a book in which the history of the past is written in every street . . . [and] the mere fact of [London's] grandeur—of its vast size—of the ceaseless stir and excitement of its daily and hourly life—is an assistance to the comprehension of History far beyond what those can have who live away from it. It raises us out of ourselves—it gives us a consciousness of nearness to the great pulses of national life.

That was Canon Arthur P. Stanley, later Dean of Westminster, lecturing in 1854 at Exeter Hall in the Strand to the young men of the YMCA, founded ten years before. Those who seek a greater 'consciousness of nearness to the pulses' of Victorian life had better

Fig. 56 *Victorian London pavement view in 1971 :*
Grosvenor Hotel, Victoria

learn to read Victorian buildings while these, with the public records relating to them, can still be read together. Like Victorian periodicals, Victorian buildings reveal a good deal about human life, and about the shape of London now, that can be learned in no other way.

Such a book as this is inevitably a personal selection, laced with personal opinions, and every reader must have pounced on omissions of favourites. These chapters are not meant to comfort either those who like to think Victorian London was altogether better than ours or those who prefer to think it was altogether much worse. It was different. And Victorians of 1837 were almost as different from Victorians of 1901 as the latter were from us. As the smoky air they all breathed was different from ours, so was the atmosphere inside their heads—their assumptions and expectations—although human nature remains much the same. This is not a potted history of Victorian architecture or of an abstraction called The Victorian City. It is a sketchy portrait of one Victorian city moving through time in a series of dissolving views—a Biograph.

Postscript 1901–14: A Victorian Legacy

A well-known Late Victorian invention that flowered in Edwardian London and elsewhere was the picture postcard, preserving like insects in amber those detailed views of the Victorian fabric that went on existing after 1901. A number of this book's illustrations are from postcards. But there were also the messages, preserving who knows what hints of anxiety or comedy or horrors of vacancy, oddments of social history too. Collectors of vintage postcards (non-seaside-comic) seldom notice the vintage messages scrawled on the backs, but these are like shreds of old conversations sometimes, makeshifts for telephones before those were common, and a boon to the scattered army of domestic servants. Perhaps only a fifty-year rule applies to reading other people's postcards?

Once again I have waited in vain, am I never going to see you! . . . meet me to-day Oxford Circus tube, yesterday's rendezvous at 6.15 p.m. I will wait 5 minutes for you. . . . I wish you yourself would write & make an appointment. . . . I don't like this uncertainty each time.
(On a view of Charlotte Street, Tottenham Court Road, to a girl in Hampstead in 1902)

I have made up my mind. I told the Butler yesterday . . . he said I only wish I was your age I would do the same, he says he has great faith in Canada, I am going to book my berth to-morrow.
(Sid, in service, writes on a view of Trafalgar Square in 1903, when *Sail away* was the rage in the music halls)

My Dear Mother just a Card to say I am coming on Monday I got a place but didn't do—Edith
(The raw housemaid sacked in Stoke Newington could only head home to her Hampshire village)

WILL you stop at home this evening for *me*, shall be round soon after 8, IF you are alone may come up again later. Please keep this view in OUR collection.
(The sender signed his full name, to a girl at a Wimbledon domestic-employment agency, where she must have been the only one to see the post, in 1905)

Dear Grannie just a card to say I got here safely a nasty yellow fog everywhere how is baby
(Battersea to Bognor in November 1906)

Dear Nurse the children can go out to Tea if you think it is allright & if Georgie has written to Miss Kate & Gladys has done some of the shawl if not they are not to go.
(Stockwell to Norfolk seaside in 1906)

Went to the White City yesterday hurried back to be in time to see that party with unfavourable result Also dissapointed this morning is it not unkind
(From Maud to Ada, 1910)

I shall be home by 6.30 get ready & have dinner ready. We shall have to hurry to get in. Cold meat and pots (fried) will do me to-night. You might rub my shoes over for me.
(Brother to sister apparently, on a view of the Army & Navy Stores, posted at lunchtime in Westminster to Rotherhithe, four miles away, in 1912)

Dear Nellie Having a grand time shall be sorry when the ends come wish it was for ever But all good things come to an end Ta Ta Flo
(From the seaside at Hastings to the North London suburb of Highbury, postmarked *2 August 1914*)

Fig 57 The Victoria Memorial, 1901, and the Victorian palace front

A Few Books

T. C. Barker and Michael Robbins. *A History of London Transport*, vol. I, 1963.

John Betjeman (ed.). *Victorian and Edwardian London from old photographs*, 1969.

Asa Briggs. *Victorian Cities*, 1968.

G. F. Chadwick. *The Works of Sir Joseph Paxton*, 1961; and illustrations, P. Beaver, *The Crystal Palace*, 1970.

Owen Chadwick. *The Victorian Church*, 2 vols, 1970.

Basil F. L. Clarke. *Parish Churches of London*, 1966.

Miles Hadfield. *Gardening in Britain*, 1960.

John Hayes. *Catalogue of the Oil Paintings in the London Museum*, 1970.

H.-R. Hitchcock. *Early Victorian Architecture*, 1955.

Hermione Hobhouse. *Thomas Cubitt, Master Builder*, 1971.

———. *Lost London*, 1971.

Peter Jackson (ed.). *John Tallis's London Street Views*, 1969.

Henry Jephson. *The Sanitary Evolution of London*, 1907.

Donald Olsen. *Town Planning in London*, 1964.

Sir Nikolaus Pevsner. *London*, Buildings of England series, 2 vols, latest editions.

Francis Sheppard. *London 1808–1870, The Infernal Wen*, History of London series, 1971. (Published too late for me to use, but amplifies much that I have only touched on.)

Sir John Summerson. *Georgian London*, 1945, final chapter.

———. *Victorian Architecture*, 1970.

——— and J. M. Richards. *The Bombed Buildings of Britain*, 1947.

E. P. Thompson and Eileen Yeo. *The Unknown Mayhew*, 1971.

Also studies of certain areas, such as: H. J. Dyos, *Victorian Suburb, a Study of the Growth of Camberwell*, 1961; H. C. Prince on North-west London 1814–1914 in *Greater London* (ed. J. T. Coppock & H. C. Prince), 1964; D. A. Reeder on Fulham 1851–1901 in *A History of Fulham to 1965* (ed. P. D. Whitting), 1970; and *Survey of London* series, ed. F. Sheppard, especially volumes on Westminster, Soho, Covent Garden, Lambeth and (to come) Kensington.

Also, of current periodicals: *Architectural History*, *Architectural Review* (mainly *c.* 1940–70 on this subject), *East London Papers*, *Victorian Studies*, occasionally *Country Life*; of Victorian periodicals, especially *Illustrated London News*, *Builder* and other building journals, *Punch*, etc. etc. And the *Wellesley Index to Victorian Periodicals* (ed. W. Houghton), vol. I, 1966; vol. II, 1972. Also, here and there, *London Topographical Record* (23 vols 1901–72).

Index

The page numbers in *italics* refer to illustrations